Tom's Story

Don't believe the lie

By
Debbie Petrie

Order this book online at www.trafford.com
or email orders@trafford.com

Most Trafford titles are also available at major online book retailers.

Printed in the United States of America.

ISBN: 978-1-4269-8173-9 (sc)
ISBN: 978-1-4269-8216-3 (e)

Library of Congress Control Number: 2011913067

Trafford rev. 12/10/2013

www.trafford.com

North America & international
toll-free: 1 888 232 4444 (USA & Canada)
fax: 812 355 4082

In memory of Tom

June 5th, 1962-September 6th, 2000

Dedicated to his mother for always being there for him.

I would like to express appreciation to the British Columbia Schizophrenic Society of Victoria. Thank you.

February 02/99
1st Day of the Rest of My Life

<u>My last 90 days:.</u> March 12/99

Tom

I have been around AA and NA for the past 11 years, realizing that I had a problem with alcohol and drugs since my first drink at age 15. Over the past years I would have short periods of sobriety lasting from 1 to 6 months, after being in jail a number of times as a result of my use. Before that I had been in a relationship with my present wife and we had a son together. I tried numerous times to clean up but it was always for all the wrong reasons, work, family, because I had a court order, because I was told to. My using brought me to the street of Victoria in 93. I was living at shelters or camping out in parks. I continued to use, especially alcohol to try to cover up all the pain I was feeling and all the resentment for people that had harmed me. This continued until 95 where I started to be introduced to the jail system. My using had been everyday for the past 3 years, in and out of jail still mad at the whole world and what it contained. Every time I would use the problem, being myself would erupt and I would be committing crime, assaulting people, and after going into a deep and dark depression. I would then go through the guilt, remorse, irrational thinking, shame and total insane thinking that I was such a worthless, piece of shit that there is absolutely no need of taking up space on this planet. I had a lot of thought of suicide and the more I thought of it the more I drank and the periods of being out of jail were getting closer together, and the feelings about me were getting worse. In November my using took me to committing 3 assaults causing bodily harm and I was looking at a lengthy jail time. I had been living with my wife and son at the time and things were getting so tense and out of control that I had left to live at the Salvation Army downtown Victoria. I had no self respect for myself, no moral values, and looking at jail again.

On November 18th I was involved in another assault and this time I was sent to jail with possibility of bail. In jail I really took an honest look at where my using had led me to and how insane I was and how crazy my life had become. Here was exactly where I wanted to be; only jail could keep me from using again. I decided to take a D&A program that was being offered, the same one that I had taken during the summer. I was told again what I had been told numerous times before but this time some of the doors of recovery started to register. I had hurt a lot of people when I was using and done things that I would not have thought of doing. I thought I had all the right intentions but started to be swayed by people who had no desire to stay clean and sober. I went for a bail hearing in December and turned down my chance at bail. I thought I needed to have a period of clean time and jail was the only way. My wife and son were very accepting of the choices I had made and when my court case came up before a judge on January 18th I was given time served plus 2 years probation.

I told my lawyer that I would just end up back in jail if I did not get some sort of help. I told him to put it in my order that I had to go into a residential treatment program for an extended period of time. I was in the process of setting this up with the D&A councilor at jail. I got out of jail and got a bed at the Salvation Army in Victoria. I ended up going back and living with my wife and son. She has 14 years of sobriety and is stable in her recovery but because of all the mental, physical and emotional abuse I had put her through over the past years I ended up trying to fix the past and everything around me. I was the problem and at fault for everything. I started to get depressed and started putting off my plans for recovery. Being totally selfish, I used on 3 separate occasions within a week. My wife had enough. I was lying to her about being absent from the house and I ended up deciding that I had to get into a treatment center. I left for the treatment center on February 1st. Full of total fear of the unknown I turned to the old way of dealing with things. I arrived drunk out of my mind. I was at the treatment center for one and a half months totally enrolled in recovery. I made my recovery #1 in my life knowing that the only other choice I was faced with was to continue to use and die or worse go through the slow death that I had been going though over the past 20 years. I had the admission of total powerlessness and control over my addiction and honesty understood that my life was and is unmanageable. I made a decision and accepted a Higher Power in my life. My self will got me nowhere. Due to unknown circumstances I had a hot drug test. I was faced with a choice again. Knowing that I have recovery but have opened up a lot past hurts and wanted recovery in my life after experiencing the benefits of it. I had to get into another recovery program. Believing there was no hope or answer I just turned it over to God. Spiritual intervention got me safely to another treatment center. I have been clean and sober for 39 days.

Step 1

Admitted I was powerless over drugs and alcohol and my life has become unmanageable.

March 13th/99

Recovery dynamics

On March 13/99 my recovery program began. Most of the studies were based on the opinion of Dr. William D. Slickworth, chief physician of a New York City hospital, specializing on the subject of alcohol and drug addictions.

He states that the two parts of human life that are affected by the disease are the body and the mind, both physical and mental.

The illness in the body is caused by a physical craving. It is a physical craving for alcohol. The indicator of an allergy is the inability to use alcohol in any form and once used the habit cannot be broken, all self confidence is lost. The reliance upon things human is great and problems become extremely difficult to solve.

It becomes a phenomenon, a great unexplainable event which as the cause of the allergy to alcohol. The manifestation of an allergy which is triggered by the first drunk, which leads to the allergic response that we have towards alcohol our lose of self confidence has formed a habit that we cannot break. Social drinkers do not seam to suffer from the allergy to alcohol, and they seem to drink without any inanity. Dr. Silkworth describes the types of drinker. There are people that can drink with out any problems, and can stop at any time. Then there are the people like us that have the phenomenon of craving, that once we take that first drink we cannot overcome this craving and it is beyond our mental control, for instance:

- Psychopaths who are emotionally unstable.
- Those that are unwilling to admit that that cannot take a drink
- Those that are entirely normal except for the effect that alcohol has on them
- And the manic depressive type

All which have one thing in common, they drink because of the affect produced by alcohol.

We treat our allergy by experiencing an entire psychic change, and once this has occurred we find ourselves able to control our desire for alcohol, and the only affect necessary being that required following a few simple rules, as well as complete abstinence.

Mental Obsession

The alcoholic will feel entirely normal in every respect, able, intelligent and friendly after a period of time they become uncomfortable, restless, imitable and discontent. They start to remember they have lost what's been worthwhile to them in their life. They start to believe that for them there is no hope, which triggers the cycle of the ease and comfort of their first drink.

For these suffering from a physical and mental obsession, he or she cannot start drinking without developing the phenomenon of craving, and as mentioned previously the only hope is entire abstinence.

In addition to the research of Dr. Silkworth, more information was shared into the lives of Bill W and Dr. Bob. I choose to keep there anonymity out of respect, but for anyone interested, information on Bill W, the founder of Alcoholics Anonymous, can be found at AA offices and treatment centers anywhere in the world. Their story has touched millions and the twelve step program has been equally successful in helping alcoholics and addicts throughout the world.

My name is Tom and I am an alcoholic/ addict in recovery applying the twelve step program. I came from a family with a back ground of substance abuse, my father, mother and sister. My drug of choice is alcohol, cocaine and pills. I started drinking alcohol (lemon gin) at the age of 15. My first experience to dope was age 20. I started smoking hash. My drug and alcohol abuse made getting along with my family very difficult.

At the age of 16 or 17, I assaulted my mother as a result of being drunk. I wanted to go to a concert. After awhile I started to loose time from school, these things were only the beginning of my problems; I had absolutely no direction in my life. At age 16-17 I started to have complete loss of memory after drinking. At the age of 18, I started to have problems in my work. I was working as a LPN at the Nova Scotia hospital and I was fired because of my behavior. My misbehavior due to abuse also got me into trouble with the law.

By the time I reached the age of 25, I had experienced my first hospitalization due to drugs and alcohol and then again after age 30. After that there were many accidents, and many visits to the hospital due to substance abuse.

My abuse was affecting me in every area of my life, physically, mentally, emotionally and financially. I started to say and do things I couldn't remember. My friendships started to decrease, I spent more time alone. I no longer had any interests. My sleep was affected. I was starting to feel a lot of guilt and very unhappy in my addiction. The amount of drugs and alcohol was increasing, as well as the fact that I was mixing all the combinations together.

I had reached the point where I needed a drink to start the day, talk to people, quit shaking or calm my nerves. When using I had no control what so ever over the amount I would take. When I honestly wanted to, I found I could not quit entirely.

At the age of 29 I made my contact with a recovery program, on my own freewill. It was at this point I began to learn alcohol and drugs are both the same. What I mean is alcohol is also a drug. I began to realize that this condition that is affecting my life is a disease, and I accepted that fact that I have an allergy to alcohol. I have begun to see how I react to other drugs the same as alcohol and I was beginning to understand why. I was beginning to realize my obsession for drugs and alcohol made it impossible for me to quit drinking or using. I could see that I could not drink or use drugs safely. I remembered how restless, irritable and discontent I would feel at times when I was not using drugs or alcohol. I cannot take a drink like a normal drinker. They can take a couple of drinks with no trouble but not me.

Step 2

Came to believe a power greater than ourselves will restore us to sanity.

Came to believe

There is a solution; part of the solution is the feeling of having shared in a common peril, the fellowship that binds us and suffering from the same illness.

The fellowship is only one part the alcoholic has to understand the facts about him, the hopeless condition of the mind and body. Our very lives as ex-problem drinkers depend on constant thoughts of others, and how we may help meet their needs. I cannot depend on fellowship alone, working the steps, and having a Higher Power in my life. I have to continuously confess any short comings, proceed in self searching and keep inventory on my pride. These are some spiritual loops given in the program that can be applied in our recovery. When practiced regularly in our program it brings about a deep and effective spiritual experience "this is God consciousness" followed by a vast chance in feeling and outlook, a new reaction to life and our own conception of a power greater than ourselves. If a person is an alcoholic or addict the only alternative is to have a vital spiritual experience, a phenomenon of a huge emotional displacement and rearrangement. All ideas and attitude are cast to one side and a new set of concepts and motives begin to dominate and go forward into a new life, or we can go back to the hell we came. This common sole dedication can only occur when we are honest and willing. It means a personality change, sudden spectacular upheavals, sudden revolutionary, transformation, profound determination, spiritual awakening/ experiences.

The truth that could save a life is a known fact that if we are planning to stop drinking there must be no reservation of a kind, no notion that some day we will be immune to alcohol.

The problem with this is that young people can not stop on their own will power, and have gone many years beyond that point and cannot leave it alone, no matter how great the necessity or the wish. There have been stories told of the old timers with 25 years of sobriety who suddenly believe they have been cured, getting back is hell if it ever happens, or maybe if we drink with milk on a full stomach. This is the insanity of the obsession, the thoughts that go on in the mind.

Another of the alcoholic dilemmas is, we had to find a power greater then ourselves which will solve our problems, a power of which we could live.

I actually learned of several types of people that might have a problem with this. In the atheist or agnostic to start spiritual progress he or she must as soon as they can lay aside prejudice. An agnostic is a person who believes in the nature or existence of God. They want to see the physical proof that exists. An atheist is a person who has a disbelief of denial of existence of God, does not believe there is a power greater than he.

As a result of this trust, belief, our decisions and actions all lead to blocks in our spiritual growth, believing cannot be compared to faith. In the beginning we must be open minded on our spiritual matters, we have to make decisions before we can begin our journey.

When Columbus began his journey to find a new world there was a superstition, tradition, a fixed idea of a round earth, as being preposterous. He trusted and believed his own ideas that the world was round. The Wright brothers believed in faith that they could fly a plane.

The fundamental idea of God is deep down inside of every man, woman and child. God can be found in human lives deep down within us and all around us.

As I have considered in step one some level of acceptance of my condition or despair, step two is primary an attitude change and has taught me techniques for facilitating spiritual growth. My belief in most things had been damaged or destroyed.

The words "came to believe" I believe means acceptance after a decision has been made, after acceptance there is an attitude change in the way I think, live, believe and to live and have peace, happiness and a sense of direction become apart of my life, by changing my behavior my attitude changes.

I went through life before with beliefs such as:

- life is difficult
- your born, you live, you die
- there are no free lunches
- you get out of life what you put into it
- you have to love yourself before another
- only children have unconditional love
- who ever has the most gold makes the rules
- when things are going good it is hard for me to accept and I usually sabotage it
- power is everything
- it's a take, take kind of world
- if I do not take advantage of a situation someone else will
- whatever bad things I do usually come back 10 fold

Today acceptance is a very big part of my life. Instead of always dissecting everything around to see "how it ticks" I just accept people, places and things for the way they are. This is a much easier approach then my old set up. I have to concentrate on myself because I can only change myself no one else around me. Today I believe there are many things more powerful then I am. For example:

- the law
- mother Nature
- the planet earth
- night and day
- God as the power greater then myself and life itself

There have been many instances in my life that I could say yes I believe a power greater than myself cared for me and helped me.

- in 1985 I had a car accident where I should have gone over a 500 ft overpass and even though I wrote off the car I escaped with only a black eye.
- In 1986 I overdosed on pills, failed suicide attempt, and awoke in a respirator in a cardiac intensive care, alive after being clinically dead for almost a minute.
- assisting in the birth of my son Devon in 1993, A very healthy baby even though I had done a lot of drugs and alcohol before he was conceived. Thankfully his mother, Debbie was drug and alcohol free. I remember grabbing him from the doctor and counting his fingers and toes. The stats are low that a healthy baby can be conceived.
- two years ago I had liver tests done, and my levels were way above normal, within a course of a couple of months they became normal. I had assumed that if I continued with my substance abuse my liver would shut down, but it did not.

I can honestly say I have always believed in an ultimate, Supreme Being that over see's my life and can guide me if I allow it and keeps me from harm. My acceptance is my big thing in allowing my Higher Power into my life I made a decision to turn my will and my life over to the care of God, accepted Jesus Christ into my life in February 1999. I pray and meditate each day for guidance, acceptance of life on life's terms, and for my fellow man.

The insanity of chemical dependency is having an unsound mind, doing the same action, drinking, drugging over and over expecting different results. To be insane means being in hell. I have made the choice to be there because I haven't been willing to accept the truth about myself. When I continue with insane thoughts I do insane actions that progressively become more insane, as a result making me more insane. I drank and did drugs totally expecting everything to be the same, finally realizing that things were becoming more insane, insanity meaning not complete.

During the last few months I have noticed many attitude changes within myself. I am open to new ideas and experiences. I have willingness to change my old habits and the way I look at other people.

I try to look at persons good qualities instead of judging them for the bad. I totally accept the way life is and life is only as difficult as I make it. I am more loving and caring towards others and not as selfish as I used to be. I appreciate the little things in my life right now I do not have any worries about the future. I just live for today. I can only deal with now and have no control over what happens later, a God of my understanding does run my life. My attitude toward life is it is very precious I do not control others I am a good person and I am deserving of my recovery.

The big book of AA says: "that God is everything or that God is nothing." God either is or isn't. The concept/idea of God as a power greater then myself, which to me is the same thing. He's totally in my acceptance instead of deciding this concept and then building it up in the way I want it to be. I have learned to accept it. I either have a total confliction towards a God of my understanding or I don't. It is all or nothing. Why would God not be everything and anything? Since this is the corner stone that holds my recovery together, I just decided that I will have the willingness and be open to this promise.

Step 3

We made a decision to turn our will and our lives over to the care of God as we understood him.

All our actions are born of our own will. our own willingness, the decisions that we ourselves in our own mind be thoughts or ideas. When we make our decisions, we choose a course of action. All decisions can be affected by making them too late or too fast.

As an alcoholic I am powerless over alcohol, therefore I choose to turn to a Higher Power, although much of the time I feel like an actor trying to run the whole show. My decision to choose a Higher Power over alcohol and drugs does not mean a thing unless it is followed by my actions. In order to accomplish this I need to let go of my will and allow Gods will to be done. Throughout the whole man kind are the only luring things that have self will.

It's our will that produces out actions, thoughts, ideas and sometimes problems. As a result we can be punished for what our self will causes others do not hurt us for no reason. Self will cannot overcome self will. We should always make our decisions with someone and not alone.

I am thoroughly convinced as of the first two steps of this program that I alone cannot overcome my addictions. Step 3 is the cornerstone of the spiritual arch. I realize my life runs on self will and can hardly be successful.

I am really starting to see the results of my past decisions and actions. I definitely feel I am at a turning point. There is absolutely no possibility of a new and different life without seeing the needs for changes, to turn my direction and my action to God. I already have the willingness to make this decision. I expected the fact that I cannot do this and only God can. I can depend upon my Higher Power to do what I can't. By being dependent on God I become more independent myself, I trust in my higher power to guide me in my life and any decisions I have to make. I rely on my Higher Power I have faith and I know it has worked and continues to work, as long as I show a willingness, except and trust in my Higher Power. Pray, meditate, and live my Gods will for me, not my self will. The doors to my recovery and my understanding things will get better, and it has.

Most of my life has run on self will and each and every time it has lead me to places and situations that I did not want to be in self will got me to where I am today, sitting in an alcohol and drug treatment center. Turning my will over to my Higher Power keeps me here. I once believed I could go out into life and take, take, take and not suffer from consequences for my actions; this has usually always landed me in jail. I believe that in my addiction I was only hurting myself, and I realized that a lot of other people that are close to me and love me are greatly affected by my actions.

I always try to run other people's lives around me thinking that I know better and I had a faster and easier way of doing things I thought I knew better. This always ended up with either my problems piling up, being put on hold or the other person would loose a lot of respect for me. When I am always looking out for fun only myself and nobody else and when only I matter and nobody else this thinking always leads me to trouble with myself and others when I am into myself and don't have any care, or consideration for anyone else. I always get hurt in the end, and then I end up feeling sorry for myself, all of a result of my own selfishness and self centeredness, self delusion all driven by one hundred types of FEAR.

Sometimes people hurt us seemingly without provocation, but we invariably find that at sometime in the past we have made decisions based on self which later put me in a position to get hurt. In my past relationships I would try to control and change a person to what I wanted them to be and eventually when the person came to their senses they would realize what I have done being totally selfish and want nothing to do with me at all again.

Numerous jobs have been a major way for me to set myself up for a fall which would leave me to all the feelings of self pity and being totally down with myself. I would get myself into a job that I did not enjoy, and go along with it and instead of just quitting I would do something stupid that would directly cause me to get fired. In the past almost 4 years hanging around with my partner in crime Bill, this friendship was totally for me, for my addiction, I was completely selfish during this time, this leading me to crash in my addiction, lose my family, job and then put all the blame upon him.

Selfishness and self centeredness being the nature of my addiction. We have to get rid of these character defects or they will kill is. To get rid of the self will that has blocked us from our contact with our Higher Power. I have to get out of myself and stop thinking that I am the be all and end all. I have to stop putting the blame on other people, places and things and look at my part in the whole thing. But turning over my self will any and all things of self that have caused me to go back to my addiction over to a higher power that I choose to call "God", I ask for Gods help in all matters concerning myself, because I have learned and can prove that my thinking got me into situations that lead me to where I am today. I ask God to do what I could not do alone. In taking this new faith I am out of self and have new concerns and interests for other people and life in general.

I already have the willingness to turn my will and life over to the care of God as I understand him. I accepted the fact that I cannot do this and only my God can. I am dependant upon my Higher Power to do what I can not. By being dependant upon God I become more independent myself. I trust in my Higher Power to guide me in my life and any decisions I have to make. I rely upon my Higher Power. I have faith and I know it has worked and it continues to work. As long as I show a willingness, accept, trust in my Higher Power, pray, meditate, and live by Gods will for me, not my self will, the door to my recovery and my understanding things will get better and it has.

Step 4

Made a searching and fearless moral inventory of ourselves

The anger toward myself causes me to be angry toward other people. My outside relationship suffered because of this I became a loner and had a tendency to judge other people.

The drugs and alcohol affected my personal relationships big time. At one point I had two separate lives; my home life (work life) and my addiction. My relationship with my wife and son suffered greatly, we separated a number of times, family court, criminal court, getting back together and separating again. If I could have remained sober and straight things would have been a lot different, a lot better.

My father affected my personal relationships, being physically abused at times I was afraid to bring friends over to the house. Even though there was sometimes when my friends did get along better with my father then I did I could not accept this and would not allow friends over to the house. There was one time in particular that I had a girlfriend coming over to the house and my father embarrassed her to the point that she ended upon the front lawn crying.

If it wasn't for the embarrassment and the unpredictability of my home life I believe that I would not have isolated myself so much that I had very few friends.

Bill was my relationship that I had for 4 years. The relationship was because of my addiction, I lived in the same hotel room he did. I made myself rely on him so much that it very much affected my relationship with my wife and son. I knew a lot of people but all of them were known by Bill too. What personal relationship, I gave up these to stick with him instead and feed my addiction.

I used to be a materialistic person at one time having things that I owned that were precious to me. I have lost most of these things and a lot has been to being to selfless, even though I cherished a lot of these things I ended up losing them usually due to my own doing. I give and give too much sometimes. I give at the expense of myself.

I lost a lot of things due to my addiction. Things have been taken or pawned off to be lost forever. The money I did make was given away to my alcohol or drugs. I have been on welfare for the past 7 years using the system thinking I was going to eventually get ahead but never did. All the things that I lost and all the things that I wanted and could not stop my addiction. I have ended up with very little, most of it being able to fit in a few boxes.

I received very little from my father. It was always my mother's responsibility for Christmas and birthdays. My father thought that his responsibilities ended with the necessities of just home and bills. I always think of him as being a very selfish man, what was his was his.

Because of my home situation and even though both of my parents worked I can always remember getting hand me down clothes and used presents. Thinking back now I can't figure out why until I think about the fact that my father had a lot of money stashed away and took my mother for the house after the divorce. My mother did struggle at times. I was forced to leave home when I was 15-16 and basically fend for myself. My money went to shelter and food until I was able to get a better job, more work hours and I could then afford the things I wanted.

I always put myself down I had pressed the self destruct button and I was off. I was worthless, could not do anything right, could not manage my own life, and was not responsible to myself. It was because of all the bad things that I did that made me a bad person and even if I did something good I had no self esteem to be able to accept it. Everyone else was always better than me. If I didn't procrastinate through everything I could have made something of myself. I had goals and dreams but these or most were not attainable because of the way I felt about myself. I had fears of success, accomplishment and acceptance from others. I was not worthy of any good feelings or of life in general. I was just existing, nothing else.

Drugs and Alcohol totally brought my self esteem down. Once a junkie always a junkie was the motto I always heard and really started to live by. I associated with using people who had only one goal in their life and it was my same goal of getting drunk and high. I feared my addiction but learned to live with the idea that this is just the way it was going to be.

I had no self esteem when it came to my father. How could I when I was always being put down and always told that

I was a mistake. It seemed to me that my father did not want me around and had a difficult time accepting me. This made me feel worthless and not wanted. In my up bringing I always thought that things could have been better. The fighting between my parents and the unstable environment at home caused me to live in a type of shell and isolate myself from other people. I felt embarrassed to have any friends over and didn't have any. I did at times feel less of myself and more on edge of what was expected of me or what was going to happen next.

My partner in crime Bill was a dream come true. He would steal all of my needs. He would steal a lot of material things for my son Devon and because Devon eventually expected these things it became hard for me to provide his expectations when Bill wasn't around. I ended up getting involved in a large number of thefts and ended up doing some time in jail.

I always believed that I was emotionally unbalanced. I could not find any centre ground and I thought I was going crazy. My depression about myself and how I looked at myself got the better of me. I was the problem and my feelings did not allow me any room to look at myself differently.

I thought of myself as a bad person doing bad things and that I would never change.

I used drugs and alcohol so I could not feel, to cover up feelings that I had about what I was doing to myself and other people. I thought I needed these things to numb myself out of all of my problems. I relied upon it, my crutch. I made myself emotionally numb as my plate filled up with all this emotional bullshit.

The only feeling I had with my father was basically fear. I would cry alone in my room a lot. I could not show a lot of emotions it was unacceptable. My father showed no emotion, accept anger. I was hurt a lot of the time but had to keep this to myself. I would be angry alone and I would take this out on myself or the wall or door. I felt at times that I had to hurt myself or be sick in order to get any kind of emotion response from my father. It was basically not being able to show any emotions and keep the so called family secret of the abuse that was going on. I can not remember any outward show of emotions between the family members. It was almost taboo to say "I love you".

With Bill all of my emotions ran on my alcoholism and addiction. The only emotion I showed was intense anger and hatred. Assault and hurting me mentally was the only thing that came out of this.

Socially, I have been basically a loner most of my life. I would have one friend and when that friendship ended I would move on to the next. My relationships were the same way. I would use that person until they were all used up and then the relationship would end usually on a very bad note and I would feel bad and shameful until the next. I did not feel part of the crowd, always looking in never out. I did not know where I fit in and always thought of myself as an outsider, so different that I was not deserving of friends. I was very selfish, using people for my needs. No parties, Get togethers, I was always the person who stood on the side lines. There was very little social aspect to my drug use. I would usually do drugs and drink alone, never into the bar scene. When I drank a lot of people around me would leave since I usually did some sort of abusive thing. I did not share very much and all I wanted to do was drink do drugs drink some more and do more drugs burry my feelings do not get in my way and pass out.

Being afraid of my father caused me to be very lonely. I can remember Cubs and Ventures but I was not involved in sports, outside activities, fishing or regular camping. I felt so much shame that I felt I did not deserve any of this. No family social events that I can remember. No family gatherings and always Christmas or special occasions were always a nightmare. They would usually end up with my parents drunk, mother crying, and father fighting with everyone and me and my sister standing there hurt and confused. I was embarrassed coming from a dysfunctional family. My parents divorced, I have had no contact with my father for over 20 years. My mother is living on the other side of Canada and I have very little contact with my sister.

Hanging around with drunk Bill and relying on him to feed my addiction caused me to isolate myself most of the time, I never hung with other people, knew a lot of people had very few friends. Embarrassed to have a friend like this, embarrassed about the situation I kept myself in.

How could a drunk and an addict have friends that did not use it was Bill and I for four years. I had scarce contact with my family little or no responsibilities. I hung around with Bill to use him for my needs. I had never experienced a type of relationship like this before. Putting all of my energy into this one person was a total waste of my life.

I had little to no security. I have only had one place of my own since I was forced to leave home at 16 years of age. I always either moved in with women, who I used, lived with my mother at home or had a room mate. I have never really had any personal belonging it was always theirs not mine. What I did have traveled with me. I moved from Halifax Nova Scotia to Victoria British Columbia with only what I could fit in my car. I did not buy furniture or house hold items because they were just too hard to travel with. Since living in Victoria I have moved twelve times, no stability, and rooming houses usually, in a tent in a park once, shared places. When I got together with Debbie we moved five times and each move usually resulted by something I did to cause the move. Debbie was always walking on egg shells, problems with rent, neighbors, and landlords. This is the way I always lived and blamed it always on the other person especially when I was causing all of the shit. All my money would go to my addiction if it was not for being on Welfare and having my rent paid direct for the past seven years I would not have a place to stay. I had to rely on a lot of times in shelters because I could not control my money. That was just the way I lived life and I could not expect anything else because of the way I lived life. I stole to live and survive through my addiction.

I had no sense of security with my father even though my needs were taken care of my emotional needs were not. We did live in the same house since I was born but I always had a sense that something could happen at any time. Being physically abused by my father at age 16 and fighting back I was put in the situation of having to leave home because I did not get along with him. I have not seen or had any contact with my father for 20 years. I don't have a father figure in my life and this effects me sometimes. I think that if things had been better in the relationship I had with my father I may have been more stable today. I remember one time my father being drunk and having a loaded gun under his bed and my mother being worried that he was going to kill us. No sense of ease or comfort there.

There was no sort of security in the way I was brought up. The only stability was in the fact my basic needs were met. There was little comfort in always worrying about what was going to happen next and when things were going good waiting for the next blow up because it was bound to happen.

Bill was forced to take care of my addiction needs. I was forced to live in his world of inability. Shit always happened when I was around him. I chose to live in shelters and hotels because this was his lifestyle and I needed him to get my wants of my addiction met.

I always needed a woman in my life. When I started dating I was very shy. I think I was always looking for someone to take care of me, a mother figure. I loved them all even though I knew very little about love. It seemed the thing to say and the thing they wanted to hear. The relationship always ended on bad terms and I would go into a deep dark depression at times even stalking them until I fell in so called love again. A dozen relationships, a dozen bad break ups. Debbie, who I am with now, I put through absolute hell. She was an enabler and that was exactly what I needed at the time. Women were always there and were easy marks at times. Now I have a lot of respect for Debbie for putting up with me for so long and thankfully still being there for me.

My father always threatened me with "you are going to grow up just like me" I swore against it and ended up proving him right. I treated women as objects, physically, emotionally abused them, just like he did to my mother. I could not talk to him about anything personal when it came to relationships. I kept it a secret from him and as far as he was concerned this was just right. The only time

I brought a girlfriend to the house he embarrassed me and her so much that she went crying out the front door. I could never forgive him for this.

What little I was taught during my up bringing, all my negative values, I carried them through the years. I thought that the way my parents treated each other was the norm and acceptable behavior. I knew no different until I was in my 20's. I tried to show caring and affection in my relationships but found it very difficult to receive.

No sexual relations in my addiction. I did not pick up girls at bars. Getting drunk and stoned did make me more courageous but I usually did very little about it. I had a "loving" relationship with alcohol and drugs. Cocaine was always the bitch that I was madly in love with and I would do absolutely everything for her. She took my life and I gave it freely. Every relationship I had, had problems because of my use of drugs and alcohol. Physical, mental, emotional abuse was the norm that was all there was to it. Since being with Debbie she has told me time after time how my addiction was destroying our relationship. Shit happened at times to cause separation but I was so wrapped up in my addiction that I did not care. Things would get out of hand or anger would erupt and I would just drink and do drugs more. I found it a perfect excuse to justify my using. That was it that was all; my addiction came first over any other thing. It ruled my life and my relationships and became an easy thing to blame my problems on.

I have been a selfish person most times. If I did not take someone else would. Take advantage of all situations because there may not be a tomorrow and the advantage may never come up again. The times I have been selfless I have been taken advantage of so even if it means hurting another person, so be it. Take, take, take, and only give back when I am going to get something in return. Most of the time the consequences did not out weigh the selfish act.

All alcoholics and drug addicts are selfish are they not? Hiding beer from friends afraid I would not have enough after that first drink. I would worry about how many I had left and how I was going to get more. It was all mine and mine only. I would steal, lie, cheat, beg my friends and especially my family to get my drugs and alcohol, rent money, food money was fair game. The more I had the more I would spend until it was all gone and then some. That was all there was to it. It was me and not very often anyone else. If I had money to spend I would spend as little as possible, as cheap as possible, and would always be working out how much I had to spend on my drugs and alcohol. This took away the promises I would make and not keep. I was always looking at the easy way of doing everything.

I guess I could have been open towards my father. I had a lot of anger towards him and shut myself off from him, because of everything that happened I did not want the father/son relationship. I could not accept the way that my father was and could only think of myself. He taught me to take, take, and take, and how shitty the world was and I took this way of thinking on as my own. At times I wanted more from him than he could give me, feelings and material things especially. I could not accept my family situation and always wanted more. I expected more at special times; birthdays, Christmas. My thinking was for all that I was going through there had to be a pay back. My needs were basically met and wants were out of control. Even now with my mother I expect a lot especially money. I believe she pays because of her guilt and my shame.

With Bill I was totally selfish. If I was going to be his friend he was going to have to pay and the price was very high at times. He would do absolutely anything I asked him to and I would take advantage of this. It was my wants that were to be met not his. He lost a lot, money, personal things, places he was living, for the good of Tom. The more I could get the more I would want. I used him so I could give to other people especially my family to make up for all the harms I did and the guilt I felt.

I basically lied to myself about how bad things really were/are. I did not want to look at myself and what I was doing. Moral values, self consciousness were out the window. I did not think that I was responsible to myself or other people. I would lie to the point of believing it myself. As bad as things were they could not get any worse, and they did. Of course I lied about my addiction. I did not see it as being so bad, even though my world was crashing down around me. I justified my using in as many ways as I could. I would lie about the fact that I was using and the amounts I was using. I would always say that I was a drinker and not a drug user. I was wrong to lie about my using and if I was honest about my using and how much my life was screwed up because of it I could have saved myself a lot of heart ache and could of saved a lot of other people from the harm I have caused them.

I do not remember being dishonest with my father. I do not remember having that much of a chance to be. He did not seem to care if I was lying or not. I stole from him only on one occasion and that was a knife. He knew I did it, I knew I did it and it was basically left at that. To lie to him was to be punished by him and his punishment out weighed anything else.

I believe my family was based on some sort of lie. There was some deep dart secret that nobody talked about. What was happening in our family was kept behind closed doors. When we left the house it was like put on your happy mask to show the world that we were alright and normal. Things were said and then never talked about again. My mother did not keep secrets about what was going on within the family with myself and my sister. I remember telling my mother that I was a junkie all she said was "don't tell me that" I think she kept it secret to every one around her exactly how bad things were. We don't admit our wrongs to anyone.

I was totally dishonest in my relationships. I lied to get what I needed all the time. Totally normal for what I was going through. I did not have remorse for what I did, not at all. It was just something I did, had to do, felt I had to do and that is it. I got caught in lies many times, was a little embarrassed by it and had another drink.

My biggest fear was myself. I had gotten to the point where I did not no how much more harm I was capable of doing. Self will run wild. I had pressed the self destruct button and was out of control. I harmed a lot of people, did things that in my wildest dreams I would not consider doing. I had a lot of fear for myself. I was very afraid of what I was capable of doing. At times I thought I had normal values or conscience. I would act without thinking, would not even consider the consequences of my actions. When life would stop me and say that what I did was wrong I would get angry and just do something worse. I stole, lied, cheated, hurt, conned, I was irresponsible, uncaring, unloving, taker, user, abuser and could be the most untrustworthy person you have ever met. A lot of the times I would feel no guilt for what I did. It seemed that as bad as I was the worse I wanted to be. I was so lost in my addiction that it did not matter how much that I took or how much I drank. I was on a total death wish. I would get myself in a lot of situations that thinking about it today I am totally surprised that I made it out of it alive. I feared what drugs and alcohol would do to me but I was so sick that it did not matter any more. I lived for my addiction and I was going to die a drunk and junkie.

I had total fear of my father. I had no respect for him but I feared the physical abuse that he was capable of doing. I would have to wait until he got home from work to deal out the punishment for the day. I was a very frightened little boy not knowing any different and having to accept what was going on because that was all I knew. I have not seen my father since I was 16 years old. I do not get in touch with him because of anger and fear of what he is capable of doing. "You are a bad person, you will not amount to anything, and you will grow up to be just like me"

I'm resentful at myself, my drug and alcohol addiction, my father, the way I was brought up, Bill. The fact that I procrastinate usually put things off. These are usually important things that should be dealt with right now. I usually let my problems build up until my plate is over flowing and then I will scramble around trying to straighten every thing out all at once. If things are going bad I make them really bad and if things are going good I cannot accept this and have to sabotage it to make it bad. I always seem to be in the wrong place at the wrong time. I know that there is no such thing as bad luck but why does shit always seem to follow me and happen around me. If I am going to get in to trouble why can't I foresee the consequences of my actions first? Can I not step back in order to see forward? I want to be able to be trouble free or at least trouble less.

Why did I ever get involved in drugs and alcohol? I experienced the affects that alcohol had on my family, the anger, violence, divorce. Even though I said over and over again I was not going to let it destroy my life, it eventually did. I crossed the line and could not come back to any form of fun that I did have in the beginning. I saw it destroying my life but continued to keep plugging at it with all the gusto I had. It was there even though I knew I was screwing up my life and the people around me, I still did it. If I could use and have no problems because of it I would that is the nature of my addiction. If the drugs and alcohol did not exist I would not have all the problems I have now. They destroyed my life, jail, psych ward, clinically dead. I wish I could have dealt with my feelings instead of relying on drugs and alcohol to cover them up and take all the pain away temporarily.

Why couldn't my father show love towards me or at least tell me that he loved me? The physical abuse the name calling, put downs, the way he treated my mother, my no self esteem. He always said that I would grow up to be just like him. This was more of a threat and it ended up turning into a revelation. He could have shown some sort of affection, let me be his son, we could of had a better relationship. Why did he put me through all of what he did? Was his childhood as bad or even worse? Didn't he learn anything and if he didn't what gave him the right to bring me into the world? I was a mistake, unwanted. I heard this all the time. What a thing to say to a child growing up. No wonder I was so screwed up and carried the same attitudes into my personal relationships. I remember some special times but they do not out weigh all the bad that happened. Abusing me with a pair of slippers at Christmas time how dare he do that. What was going through his head at the time, did he have a conscience, any moral values, guilt for what he did. Putting my mother through hell carrying all that hatred around and dumping it on everyone, just because he was mad at the situation he found himself in of having to support a family did not make what he did right.

I know all families have problems but I always believed that ours had secrets as well, still don't know what they were or if there was any I just had a feeling that they were there. I can say if things were better, if there was more love, values, closeness, less problems, acceptance, I would have grown up to be a better person. Instead of being totally screwed up, always being told what was right then my mom and dad proving to me that they didn't have to follow the rules. The fighting between my sister and myself and the very little contact I have had with her over the years. I moved from Halifax, NS just getting as far away as possible from them. I have two nieces I never seen and my mother has never seen my son and I haven't talked to my father in 20 years. The family that was there is no longer. If we all had of known what the future was going to be I bet we would not have made the choices that we did.

I am fearful at myself, relapse, going back to that hell, being part of my family, partner to my wife Debbie, father to my son Devon. I fear life, success, the future. I fear what I am capable of doing. All the evil things I have done, not having a conscience or any moral values.

I fear going back to the life style I came from, the self destructiveness where drugs and alcohol had brought me. The fact that at some time I am going to have one of those blank moments in my thinking and not realizing that I have been in a relapse mode anyways, find myself loaded. Am I responsible enough? Can I care and love two people that are so important in my life right now. Will I cause something that will make me lose my family again? I fear where I will be and who I will become. Will I be able to be a productive person in society?

I fear for the way I was brought up. Fear made me stay away from my family as much as possible. I did not want to submit myself to the bull shit that I went through. Why should I put myself through any more? They are on the other side of Canada and that is the best place for them. This way I have the control that I did not have most of my life.

The only fear that I had for Bill was the fear that he would leave and I couldn't get my wants met. If he left I would be forced to steal and cheat to get what I wanted at the time. He provided the drugs and the alcohol and everything I needed to make amends, even though they were always material, to the people that were the closest to me that I had harmed.

I did not care about myself or even loved myself. The way that I lived proved this. I have spent the last 10 years living in shelters, hostels, camping in parks, living in dumpy hotels, rooming houses with people who were in their addiction just like me. Everything that I have stolen, I did not take care of myself even though I tried. The way I was living was not in my plans for my goal in life, on welfare, scamming the system, living totally on the edge, hating myself for the person that I had become.

My actions were inconsiderate in my addiction, take, take and take some more. My addiction came first over food, shelter, friends, work, and family. I had forced myself into a bad situation drugs and alcohol would always be there. All the worst part of my character would come out. I became this evil being capable of almost anything. Everything I did was for my addiction and I did not care who or what got hurt in the process.

I was not considerate of my father; I had no respect or love for him. He was just the person who came around once in a while, paid the bills and put food on the table. I think at times he wanted better for me but I didn't care. I did not even consider his feelings when I made the decision not to have any contact with him. If I could have gotten through all of the anger and hate that I felt for him it may have totally changed the chance of us having a father/son relationship.

I was not the son that my parents wanted me to be. I did not consider my parents feelings or my sister's. Everything appeared to be free game to me and I took full advantage of it. My mother was put through a lot because of my actions and decisions. Missed birthdays, Christmas, no contact for long periods of time, and when there was contact I would always need something. It was always, look at me and all the difficulties I am going through, because of all the problems I cause.

Myself, I believe that I do not have my self-esteem or self-worth. I do not consider myself a good person. I do not love myself and sometimes I believe that I am not worthy of having a place in society. I constantly put myself down for the position I have got myself into, how I lead my life, who I had become, what I have made of myself, what little I have done, the people I have harmed and the wrongs I have caused. I look in the mirror sometime and I don't recognize the reflection back. Sometimes I do not know who I am and what position I have to lead. I am down on myself; I have no realistic goal set, and a lot of what I do want to do in life I do not attain.

Relapse scares the hell out of me. I do not know if I have what it takes to make it, or if I can. I do not want to go back to where I came from, that slow death. I do not want to do the things I have done in the past. Do I really have what it takes to live a life of total abstinence? Am I going to make it and keep my family? I have lost them a few times in the past and do not want that to happen in the future. My family has always counted on me. Responsibility was always very hard for me. I let them down so many times and they tried to stay with me hoping that I would get better. I have stolen from my wife; I have assaulted her on 4 different occasions. I have brought her down made her mentally and emotionally sick. I took away a lot of her hopes and dreams. I have been irresponsible with my son. I believe at times that I have been a really bad partner and father, and I have used the situation to the utmost. I have done things that I can not believe that I have done, and Debbie and Devon have stood by me and loved me through thick and thin, through all of the bad stuff. I was always part of, not part of my family. I still cannot believe that I have a wife and son and that I have not lost them.

I am worthy of success. I can not see myself In the future. I can have some goals about how I want things to be and can attain them. Will my life be full of happiness? Will I become my own success? I do not know if this is possible or if there is still time left. All the wrong that I have done and I do not know if life is possible all I want is to be happy, comfortable, a family unity, and hopefully I do not screw it up to the point that I will never have a chance again.

I have been around NA for 11 years, always wanting recovery but never recovered. I knew exactly what I should do but never doing it. I always went back to people who used because these were the people I was more comfortable with.

I found it hard to have relationships with recovering people because I knew that at some time I would let them down. I wanted these people as friends but I did not deserve them. Always went back to my addiction and dragged someone down with me.

I'm still a loner even in relationship with my family. I had no good friends and the ones I did have were people that I would not bring home. I tried to have two lives; family, addiction, two responsibilities; family man, addict. This did work for a while and then things started to mix together. Family life went. Addict friends were always there.

If I hung around positive people I would have a positive attitude that is all there is to it. The life I lead in my addiction was the lifestyle I had. I hung around a lot of people who were going absolutely no where. They had no goals and were only looking for the drugs and alcohol to fill there needs for the day. This is who I also became. I remember high school where most of my friends had plans for living. I chose to have what I believe to be a freer more carefree lifestyle. I paid the consequences in the end. I have a lot of regret for not making the right choices back then. I might not be where I am today.

Like I have previously mentioned I have never really been a materialistic person. What I own I basically can travel with. It's light so I can move fast, why? because I have always been on the move most of my life. Pick up and go when the shit is coming down, my escape route, my way out. Nice and quick and easy. I wanted things in my life but most of them were too heavy to move. Maybe if I had some materialistic things in my life it would give me one more positive thing I can look at if I do get into a relapse mode. Anything of value I did have was either lost or pawned off. I looked at it as only another form of money to supply my addiction.

I moved into a very furnished life with Debbie, she owned everything I owned nothing. Even though she always told me that it was ours I always thought of it as hers and her place. I give my son a lot of things, presents, but they are given only as a way of saying I am sorry for all of the hurt I have put him through. Oh! It would be so nice to own a house, a car, furniture and even a few toys. This is not the only thing that would make me happy; it is just a small part of it. To be comfortable and settled in life. To have some of my wants met. I guess the future is still up for grabs.

I have a fear of being emotionally unstable, to be insane and not able to come back. The way I acted insanely made me do insane things. I have done things that only an insane person would do. What if I did not come back from the way I thought in the past? I am slowly changing and fear going back to that thinking again.

I used my addiction to cover up all the feelings that I had because of all of the shit that I have put myself through. I could not feel anything but quilt, shame and remorse. Now I am experiencing a wide range of emotions and worry that if it does become to overwhelming that it may cause me to go back to that numb place that I came from. Showing emotions is a good place for me right now. I deal with my feelings when they come up and do not allow them to get to overwhelming.

Emotionally I am pretty numb when it comes to my family. I can a lot of the time verbally express my feelings but have a very hard time showing them. My feelings can get right out of control and a lot of the time it is feelings of anger. I know what I am capable of and it scares the shit out of me. I want to have balance with my feelings. I want to be happy and content.

Can I calmly walk through life on my journey in my success and not get bent out of shape emotionally? Hopefully I can deal with things as they come up, because I know that not to have some sort of balance I am doomed to repeat failures.

I fear that I will not find a positive group of people to hang around with. My biggest thing is being a loner if I do not have friends in recovery and treat this friend with trust and dignity that they deserve I will lose them, go back to being a loner and there is a very good chance that I will relapse. I do not know how to handle myself around other people. I usually put on some sort of mask that I would think that these people would like to see. I do not know myself at all. I do not seem to fit in at all. I know I fit into recovery though.

I know that I will not be accepted socially if I go back to my addiction. I hung around people who did the same thing I did. I thought it was normal to drink first thing in the morning. I thought the rest of the world was doing what I was. Relapse is not socially acceptable for me because I have come too far and if I relapse there will be no hope.

I fear my mutual friends getting in the way. I fear sharing my family with others, having others finding out about my addictions and being judged. I will need new friends who are not using, good people in my life, a healthy lifestyle a new way of life. My future must be good, satisfying and rewarding. I must be selfless and have goals that are aimed to helping others. If I do not chose this way I may as well go back to the hell I came from.

Will I be comfortable and settled, will I have possessions and cherish them, can I hold on to them. Will I have peace of mind and stability in my life and balance? Will relapse take everything away that I have and will gain in recovery? Do I have the strength, will I ever have complacency. Relapse will take me directly back to a hell that I know too well, it will be 100 xs worse. I do not want to lose everything again. My family has hope for the last time.

Will I still have my freedom when it comes to my family? I want to be a part of and still be my own person. I have a tendency to get so wrapped up in someone else that I can lose myself in the process. I have to be able to draw the line, find a balance and establish boundaries and stick with them. The future holds a lot of fears for me. Can I make it, will I end up content and safe. I do not want to go back to the life and lifestyle I came from. That life was barely maintaining. I am a better person than that and deserve better than that. I cannot raise a family and have recovery without a stable life. Will my future contain these things? I hope and I pray.

I can be a very selfish person. I can take, take and take. I sometimes believe that I give in order to receive it most of the time does not come back. All the drugs are mine, everything is mine. There is absolutely no sharing. Fuck the rent, food, bills, family, myself, and any body else. All my money went to the addiction, all your money went to. That was the way I was I would take all that you had and then some. That was me in my addiction.

I try not to be selfish with my family. I try to provide, for the last few years I have been on welfare and doing crime so I provided very little. A lot of it would be from stealing, scams, food banks, etc. I could sometimes get away with this. It was the only way I could think of. I could have spent more time with them but I did not. Selfish, there were promises that were not kept, especially with Devon when Debbie and I were separated he would wait for one of my promises to be kept and sometimes they weren't. Not even with an explanation at times. He was very hurt and confused which made me very guilty.

If I do not open up to new ideas and remain self-centered I will not make it in life. Sometimes life can be such a difficult thing when all I do is want. I can walk on people to get my wants met and not even care. I guess if I put a healthy approach to success and the future I can get a lot of my needs met without hurting people along the way.

I can be very dishonest with myself. I can lie about something to the point of believing it myself. I lie to myself about how bad things really are and have become. I can lie about the past and present to make it appear to be either better or worse to someone else. Sometimes I can lie without even knowing that I am lying. I fear the truth. I do not want to get to the point where I am in the process of the thinking and feeling of relapse and I can not be honest about what is going on. Hopefully when and if this point comes I can recognize all the signs before it is to late.

I lie to my family on a regular basis, money, jobs, where I have been, what I have been doing, who I have been with, how clean I have been. When I first met Debbie I lied to her about being a nurse. I have lied to Devon about not drinking when he asked me to promise him. I hope I can have realistic goals about the future.

I am frightened of myself and what wrongs I am capable of doing. I do not admit fault or wrongs very often or own up to my own shit. I can blame someone else before myself. I do not know exactly what I am capable of doing in a good way. I know I can be a very generous and kind person. Can I truly recognize exactly how bad things really have become? I am a very sick person in my addiction. It's like I turn into Mr. Hyde, I project a black aura when I am using, a side of me that I do not wish to see again.

I have lost a lot of trust because of the things I have done in the past. Debbie and Devon can walk on egg shells sometimes waiting for the next out break of problems. I am unreliable; trust is a big issue with me. I can trust someone else because they can be trusted. It will take a long time before my family will ever fully trust me again. Trust will be a slow process and I have to accept it. Admit when I am wrong, admit my shortcomings, be selfless, do onto others as I would want done unto me, admit my part in it. If I can accomplish these things my future has no boundaries, I can become whatever I put my mind to and I can understand myself a lot more.

I have to be considerate to other people, recognize other people's boundaries and not go over them. I need to be more loving towards myself instead of always putting myself down, not loving myself, not thinking that I am worthy of being alive and enjoying life. I have to be very selfish about my recovery. It is only by the Grace of God and the way that I work his will for me that I am able to make it today.

I have to be part of my family. I have to respect their boundaries as I would want them to respect mine. I have been very inconsiderate of their feelings in the past and I have to stop and recognize that. My goals in the future have to include the people in my life that are important to me. I can not walk over people like I have done in the past.

Who did I harm?

- Myself
- Debbie
- Old girlfriends

With myself, inappropriate behavior and actions, thinking that I was better than anyone else, that I was the only one that could do it. I would have to fix it in the end myself. I was involved in a relationship with a partner in crime. I forsake my family for what I was involved in.

Debbie I took away all her self-esteem and worth she became stagnate in her life. She lost all of her goals. She was so involved in all of the bullshit I was going through that she actually got physically sick, mentally she had to increase her medication and go on an anti-depressant, emotionally she lost control, and spiritually she had lost contact with her Higher Power.

Most of my old girlfriends I treated the same way. I controlled and used, I tore down and built them up to be the person I wanted them to be. I used them materialistically, always moving in with them with nothing, owning everything that they had.

I did not at a time know where I stood sexually. I had a fear of women and insecurity about them. I loved them to pieces but I always felt that it was control or be controlled. I did a lot of mean things that really brought me down, very little that I was proud of used women to feel superior about myself. I had such low self-esteem that I had to be some power person and control them.

Because of the care and concern my mother had for me I looked for this in other women.

Debbie took care of me, because I couldn't take care of myself, she picked up the pieces, picked me up off the floor, physically and mentally. I took her self-esteem as my own.

I destroyed a lot of girlfriends out there, low self-esteem, used a lot of people used, used, used, take, take, take. Felt bad about what I was doing I would set a situation up to all hell would break lose so I could drink and use drugs.

I never had any real positive personal relationships. I did not want people in my life that knew what was going on. At one time work involved working with women (nursing) and since I had a fear and was uncomfortable with women it was a perfect arrangement for me.

I did a lot of harm to Debbie there was a lot of inappropriate behaviors. I embarrassed her at times but I continued on at it. I think it was a lot to do with controlling. I did not allow her to have any girlfriends and was always jealous when she had any male friends. My insecurity caused all of this.

Emotionally I was a wreck. I had used drugs and alcohol for so long that I was very numb, either high and running all over the place doing a million things at once and only accomplishing a few, or depressed about myself and the guilt, shame and harm I had caused. I hung onto women for emotional support or cause shit so we could always be feeling the same thing at once.

With Debbie she started out being my rock. I thought of her as being a firm foundation for me to grow on, a new start. She got just as sick as me by being totally wrapped up in my problems she did not know who she was. I hurt her emotionally, physically, and mentally. Name calling, put downs, making her feel the shame that I felt. I totally drained her emotionally and still made her go through it some more. I love you and will never do that again, became my favorite saying. She would kick me out of her house but she could not get me out of her life. She stood by me waiting patiently for me to become healthier. I am very grateful that she is still in my life today when I have become a healthier, better person. All of my relationships have been the same, emotional abuse, exactly the same thing that my father had done to my mother. I would yell, they would cry, and then I would say that I was sorry. This would go on and on until the relationship would break up and then I would feel sorry for myself, blame them for all my problems and then have so much anger for them that I would never see them again.

I was not secure in myself that is why I moved into a women's secure environment. I relied on them because I could not make it and if I tried I found it very difficult on my own. No stability without being in a relationship. I found it very easy to bounce around from relationship to relationship. Someone always had to be taking care of me and healthy enough to take care of them self. That is why I did not get involved in any relationship where the other person was as sick as I was. I did not see anyone who drank or did drugs. I wanted it all and did not want to share. I needed someone to pick up the pieces after I screwed everything up.

Debbie took care of everything, the rent, the bills, the worries, the problems, my problems. She was very responsible and I took full advantage of this. This gave me reason to use, gave me reason for my cons and scams and my thieving. I always had a secure place to go to I had no worries I could usually con my way back into the house. That usually ended up not working any more. She would worry about the neighbors, the eviction notices and at times I could put all my effort into the problem it just made using the next time justifiable.

It was the same with all my past relationships. I would move into a secure environment until they either lost everything or got so sick of all the new problems that arose from it,

I was afraid of being alone. I felt that only another woman in my life would fill my loneliness, the empty hole that I had inside of me. I did not like myself and who I was. I used women to get my needs and wants met.

I was frightened of losing Debbie; we actually have spent more time apart than together. She stood by me in my addiction, in my crisis and when I was in jail. She actually saw some hope in me when I saw no hope in myself. She knew I was a good person and it took me a long time for me to realize why she had to let go. I was dragging her down. When we split up the first time I just used it as a good opportunity to drink and use drugs, since she was sober when I met her I could not use around her. I am afraid of losing her but I know that I can now survive on my own.

Past relationships were the same. I was developing so much insecurity that when the relationship ended I would go into a deep dark depression. I first try to get the other person back, making promises that she wanted to hear and when it did not work I would be very angry and resentful and almost to the point of getting back at the other person.

I was inconsiderate to myself about what was really going on in my life. I did deserve someone in my life that was going to love and care about me as long as I gave this back to them. With Debbie I was inconsiderate about just about everything, her feelings, her needs, and the affection that she needed and even craved at times. As long as my needs were met it was not important for my partners to have there needs and wants met.

Who did I hurt?

- Myself
- Debbie/Devon
- Society-Stealing and Conning
- Elderly/Handicapped
- My family

What did I do?

- I was not open to new ideas; I did not live up to my full potential.
- I did not maintain a healthy lifestyle. I did not recognize the full extent of my problem with drugs and alcohol.
- I procrastinated over the simplest things always putting off even major things until they piled up and when I could not handle them I went back to the comfort of drugs and alcohol.
- I remained on welfare for the past 7 years, never working or setting goals and making an attempt to attain them.
- I poisoned my body and burnt out a lot of brain cells through my addiction.
- I got Hepatitis C through my use.
- I became depressed and suicidal.
- Even though I sought help for my addictions I did not listen to any suggestions.
- I allowed my self to be involved in situations without looking at the consequences.
- I emotionally, physically, and mentally abused Debbie. I abused her to the point of breaking her teeth, blacken her eye, broke her glasses and pulled hair out of her head.
- I stole from her, cheated on her, lied about everything; I did not live up to my responsibilities. I left her carrying the load and mending our life.

- I abandoned her for days in a row.
- I did not respect her wishes.
- I used her, manipulated the situation, and turned it around to make it seem that it was her fault.
- I hunted her when we were separated.
- I took away her freedom, friends, security, dreams and goals.
- I was not a responsible father to Devon.
- I yelled at him, spanked him, and ignored him when I was going through all my shit.
- I stole things to give to Devon to make up for all the harm (emotionally) I caused him.
- I reneged on my promise to not drink after much asking on his part.
- I made promises that I did not keep.
- I went out with him and ended up drunk or stoned when he was with me.
- I missed two birthdays and two Christmas's because I was in jail.
- I caused him shame by putting him down.
- I could and should have shown him more love.
- I stole from just about everywhere and anyone.
- I scammed a church out of thousands of dollars.
- I ripped off the government by falsifying taxes.
- I ripped off welfare by lying.
- I scammed ICBC by writing a check that bounced for my insurance.
- I scammed UIC
- I got a student loan and never paid it back.
- I have done a number of bank frauds with empty envelopes.
- I have ended up in prison through my actions relating to my addiction.
- I have stolen things and resold them.

- I have used people, places and things for my own selfishness.
- I have worked in nursing with the elderly for over 15 years.
- I lost my empathy the last time I was working. At that time I stole money and jewelry and personal affects from them.
- I abused them mentally and emotionally.
- I lost any respect for the elderly, and just considered it a job nothing else.
- I had little care for their comfort and well being.
- I stole a lap top computer from one nursing home I worked in.
- I broke into a safe in a group home and stole all the residents' money.
- I was suspected of a lot of things but it could not be proven.
- When my sister lost her baby I did not console her.
- I did not help her out when she could have needed me.
- I did not keep in contact with her except once a year; I sometimes did not recognize her birthday or Christmas.
- I fought with her as a teenager and hurt her, stabbed her in the head with a fork.
- I left my mother to move from Nova Scotia to Victoria, I do keep in touch with her now but before it was very erratic.
- I have conned her out of money for my addiction.
- I have caused her to worry about me and feel shame and responsible for the way my life is going.
- I was not there when she was going through the divorce with my father.

- I have not seen my father in 20 years. I have only tried to call him once and sent him a father's day card when I was in treatment in 1991, forgiving him.
- I blame him for most of my problems.
- He has not seen my son and I do not know if he even knows he exists.
- I do not know if he is alive or dead.
- I have let him go completely,

I have put myself down to the point of no self-esteem or worth. I hate myself for getting involved in drugs and alcohol fully knowing the affects of it growing up. I put myself into situations that I should have walked away from. I have harmed myself physically by suicide attempts in '86 and slicing my wrist in '94 and injecting a pesticide into me in '93. I thought I would always be a junkie and a drunk and live on skid row, exactly where I ended up.

I could not accept my families love and caring for me. I did not believe that I would make a good partner and father to my son. I put myself down constantly for what I did to them in my addiction. I gave them up when I gave up on myself.

I was a criminal and even though a got caught and went to jail I was successful all the other times. It was my wants with no regard to anyone else.

I hurt old people because I was hurt myself; I took the anger of my life out on them. I had no respect for my self so how could I have respect for any one else.

I believed that I was such a bad person and was never going to change, that I cut off all ties with my family; I hurt them indirectly without knowing it. I chose to be a loner because my thinking was that I was only harming myself. It turned out that the truth was that I took a lot of other people down with me. I could not accept people having genuine concern for me. I stayed away from a lot of people because If I was such a bad person, a liar, thief, cheat I was going to use that person to the fullest. I did not trust myself in personal relationships.

Debbie could just maintain the rent, food and bills that is about it. She had to struggle at times and she would go with out to give to Devon and myself. She was very selfless, what was hers was mine and what was mine went to my drugs. She wanted things, better things but because of my addiction she was forced to go without. I provided Devon with all his personal material needs. Since I was feeling so much guilt he reaped the benefits of my bullshit. I was very selfish when it came to providing for my family.

People lost so I could gain. I could justify just about all my actions because it was me against society and if I wanted something I took it. Life dealt me such hardships that it was my way of getting back. I used my mother for money and I did justify it for all the shit and tough times I went through during my childhood. I know now that this was very wrong and that it was just my selfishness for my addiction. I made things out to be that I was in some sort of crisis and I desperately needed her help.

I was emotionally screwed up; not knowing which way was up. I was either very high, happy or very depressed. I did not look at the real problem or I knew what the real problem was and just did not do anything about it. Debbie and Devon were and emotional wreck, walking on egg shells, not knowing what was going to happen next. When times were good they were very good, when times were bad they were hell. We are all planning to seek professional help when I leave the treatment center.

I cannot imagine how I have hurt some of the people I was paid to work for. Morally I did not even consider the consequences of my actions. How much I have stolen that has affected another person's life. My mother went through a lot of worry wondering where her son was and if I was still alive. I would not talk to her in months and months. She must have aged quite a few years in my addiction. She would always give me hell and tell me to stop the self pity and get off my ass and do something about my problem.

I could only control one person at a time and had little control of myself so it was all put into the other person. I ruled and controlled Debbie. I would go on runs lasting up to seven days where I would disappear from her, I would be afraid of phoning her because of all the guilt and shame. This arose a lot of insecurity and confusion in her to what I was up to and who I was with and if I was fooling around on her or not. Women were meant to be used and that was all there was to it. I did not care who you where, I took from you always.

I never did look at myself as being any better than what I was. Once a junkie always a junkie, I did not try to give myself a chance. I took a lot of things for granted I did not care who I hurt or how they were going to be affected by my actions. I did not consider how I would live with the consequences of my actions. With Debbie and Devon I sometimes knew that my actions would cause them harm but I was so lost in my addictions that I did not care. They were hurt very much and I would feel a lot of guilt and shame but I would continue on doing what I was doing. As long as my wants were met I did not care who I hurt or ripped off. All or nothing was my motto, and take a few people down with me. I would literally walk on people's toes to get what I wanted I would go into a place and if I saw something I wanted I took it.

I was afraid of what I was capable of doing to myself and other people. I was scared of what I had become, and the bad things that were going on in my life and how many people I have affected by my actions. I had harmed and hurt Debbie and Devon in so many ways I have done things to other people that I can not believe that I have done. I have brought Devon into situations that I thank God that he was not hurt. I hated society for what it was doing to me, without realizing what I was doing to society. I was frightened of what I had become and what more I could do. I had done some evil things and become an evil person. It scares the hell out of me. How could I have done some of the things that I did? The evil men do. How I have hurt a lot of people by my actions. It had got to such a point that I had taken myself out of working in nursing it scares me to think of how much more harm I am capable of doing. I have hurt my mother, I can remember a couple of instances where I hurt her physically. I had taken much abuse from my father growing up that I just snapped at the age of 17 and beat him up. I am very frightened of what I have become.

I can be a better person if I just let myself be. I do love myself if I allow myself to be loved. I am a caring person, I can be a good partner, and father. I have to consider my own feelings, emotions, admit my mistakes and my part in things. I have to be accountable for my own actions. I have to consider Debbie and Devon's feelings and there boundaries. I have to respect where they are and what they do not want in their life. I need to be considerate of other people and change my old ways of thinking. I cannot take and take and not consider the consequences of my actions. I will treat the elderly with respect. If I can not do this I do not have a place working with them. I have to be considerate of their place and their boundaries. These are the people I have learned the most from. I need to be considerate of my family for who they are. I cannot put blame on them for who I have become in my life. They are not at fault, they are accountable for their own actions and most of it is because they knew no difference from the ways and values they were brought up with.

Step 5

Admitted to God, to ourselves, and to another human being, the exact nature of our wrongs.

I had a lot of shame and guilt for what I did in the past. A lot of it was just what I learned from my parents and what they learned from their parents. Their values were taught to me. I am sorry for all of the wrongs that I committed. I have been able to actually forgive myself for a lot of my actions and have made myself very accountable for what has happened in the past. I was a very sick person in my addiction, insane person doing insane actions. My past is in the past there is nothing I can do about it. These things happened and even though I wish that they did not occur, I forgive myself for them. I am changing my attitude and am willing to change and that is the best I can do.

I feel a great sense of relief since I have done an inventory on myself.

I have been carrying around a plate of past wrongs that has been over flowing.

There is relief from all of the pain and guilt, the sense of relief from finally being able to honestly admit all of this to myself, God, and another person.

I used alcohol and drugs to cover up most of my feelings. I was suffering from a great deal of pain from the past. I either had a great deal of anger to what I believed were the wrongs of society or guilt for the wrongs that I committed. When I could not deal with emotions I used, this was about the only thing I knew of to deal with a lot of my overwhelming feelings. I blew things wildly out of proportion. Little things became big things, and big things were put on my over flowing plate. A lot of the time I was emotionally numb .I had a hard time in recognizing a lot of emotions and when strong emotions would come up I would hide them with drugs and alcohol. Anger, hurt and fear were normal emotions for me; I could recognize these things very well because these were a product of the life style that I was leading. My self will, my feelings instead of Gods will for me.

I am not the be all and end all of the past, that was my attitude in my addiction, and it did not work then so it is surely not going to work in my recovery. I am more aware of my faults and when I recognize these I try not to commit any action that might hurt another person. I am making amends for my wrongs, attitudes and actions. With my wife I have recognized my control issues, and my better than you attitude. I know that I have a lot of work to do and have the willingness to make the changes in myself.

I have turned my will and my life over to my "God" I recognize the fact that I have to make a total change in my ways and thinking of the past. Old ways did me no good. Even only being in recovery for a short period of time I see the promises of a new and rewarding life. I have no fear in the future and as long as I have a willingness to work hard and change my thinking, work my program to the best of my ability, the sky is the limit. I trust in my Higher Power to put me in the right direction on the path of recovery, Why in the hell would I want to go back to my old ways of thinking when this is what I have wanted for so long, recovery , and I basically did not know how to go about attaining it. If I started going back to my bad ways of thinking, attitudes, ways of doing things, these that had no benefits except to survive in my addiction, will eventually cause old patterns and feeling to come back and I WILL relapse back to the hell I came from. I accept people, places and things for exactly what they are, no control issues, and the only thing I can change is myself.

I have a lot of joy and happiness in my life right now. There is a sense of relief and contentment in what I have accomplished so far. I have been searching for happiness and peace for so long not able to recognize the fact that these feelings were always there I just had covered them up with alcohol and dugs. I have accomplished a lot so far in my recovery. I love myself and know that I am a good person. I honestly know that what I have now and this positive feeling can be taken away from me the instant I make that choice to go back to my addiction. I pray that for today I will have the conviction to make it and each day in recovery is one more day that I and my Higher Power have.

I do obsess on the idea of recovery and the happy and full filling life and promises that are contained within. I have a conviction to "make it" and still hold the idea that I will do absolutely everything it takes. I have made some big time changes in my life and attitudes. If I do not live in the solution by working my program I know absolutely what will happen, relapse. That is not an option for me. I do what it takes and recognize when I am in my slippery thinking. My brain has a definite contract out on my ass. It is my thinking, rationalization, and justification that will get me back out there.

I have a Higher Power in my life that I trust and love, willingness and a strong stable foundation in my recovery; I can now recognize character defects and work on these on a daily basis. I know right from wrong feelings and actions. I have acceptance and know that I don't have to own someone Else's shit and attitudes. These things are of the past, I will never be perfect, but more patient, tolerant, understanding, and caring. I have no overwhelming anxieties, just a sense of contentment and peace, and a sense of being on the right path. I hope and pray that these feelings carry on and when problems with life and when conflict and life deals me a hard blow that I will have the conviction to make it through. I see myself growing and look forward to more growth in the future, spiritually, mentally, and emotionally.

I pray and meditate on a daily basis and have been doing this for over two months. I have accepted a Higher Power into my life and have turned my will and my life over to my Higher Power. In the morning I give thanks and pray for patience, tolerance and acceptance. I pray for people in recovery and those that have made the choice to remain in there addiction. I pray that my family will be safe and that we might all have a happy day. During the day when problems and concerns come up I pray for direction and the ability to have acceptance of people places and things and to know that I can not change or control these things. Peace and understanding are what I strive for in my recovery.

Prayer helps quiet the anxieties in confusing times and there is a great sense of relief in knowing that I do not have to do this alone, that my Higher Power in my life is the only thing that can help me, to have something to turn my will over to and know that I will get direction from my Higher Power. Direction can come in a form as even a new understanding, or new way of looking at the situation. It has been proven to me over the last few months that prayer does work. I can quiet my mind and relax knowing it is as bad as only I make it out to be. It will and has to get better and it will never get as bad as it used to be as long as I do not take my will back and make that fatal choice of going back to my addiction, it's as simple as that.

Admitting my shortcomings is a behavior I have had to learn. The only time that I have ever admitted a wrong that I have committed is before a judge with my lawyer present and these were only half truths to begin with. Only if I am caught would I admit any thing in the past I would admit things if I am forced to and if by my admission there is something for me to gain in the process. That was the past. Now I admit when I am wrong and make the appropriate amends. I admit not knowing everything and not knowing all of the answers. All of my knowledge is from experience (learned) and from what other people have taught me. It is my act of being humble and not having to carry any more baggage around with me like before. It's a sense of relief and contentment and being happy with myself I am far from perfect and will never be.

I admitted to the group that I had stolen some items from Value Village the first week in the treatment centre. I made amends to the people I had put in jeopardy and to the treatment centre itself. It was a very humbling experience not knowing what the consequences of my actions were going to be. A character defect that I know now could very well have jeopardized my recovery. The admission was a true acknowledgement of my wrong in actions and in thinking. Any thing I am going to do in a positive way is going to be a benefit in my recovery. I took the action in admitting my wrong and in resolving this I made my amends to the people it directly affected. I was afraid of making this admission but with my Higher Power there was no fear. This makes me a healthy person making healthy life choices.

I had no fear in my admission of my resentments, fear, sex conduct and harms. It was the first time that I was totally honest with myself and honest with someone else. I knew that in order to further my journey along in recovery I was going to have to admit all my wrongs. The first time was a little nerve wracking but practice does make perfect. I have caused myself and others a great deal of pain through my actions in my addiction.

I knew my life was unmanageable and I was the cause and problem of all of the kayos. I have no problem in admitting this honestly. I have this new gift of admitting responsibility for my actions, my old ways of keeping things in , fears, hurts, hopes and dreams did not work I have a sort of trust in myself and a new trust in other people. Trust can be gained as well as lost.

People can not think any less of me now and any admission on my part is an improvement. There is honesty and there is cash register honesty and as long as my honesty is not going to cause someone grievous harm so be it. What a change in being a totally dishonest person who would lie to the point of almost believing it my self. I will try my hardest to be an honest person. It makes me feel good in changing one of the greatest character defects that I have. I have a sense of relief and accomplishment.

My Higher Power knows of all my rights and wrongs, I am definitely aware of this. Admitting my difficulties to God was an honest admission of my self and saying it to another person confirmed it to God also. It felt like a cleansing, never been baptized, but I believe it would be the same thing. I ask for help and give thanks for good times and even though the answers are indirect a feeling of peace and calm comes over me. I am forgiven for the past.

I have been looking forward to admitting my difficulties to myself for many years. I have been carrying this plate of hurts around for so long, and did not know how to deal with it. I have been dishonest with people around me and so dishonest with myself that I could not get any release so I covered it all up with drugs and alcohol. I had to admit my faults and share in the problems of the past, and be able to go on and be able to be very comfortable living in the present; today, the solution. This is one of the greatest personal accomplishments I have made. I am actually very proud of myself for the work I have done so far.

The word admission to me means to surrender, to humble myself, to admit my part and my fault in all matters. By my admission I clear the wreckage from the past, clear the slate. All the energy it took to keep all of this inside, all of the embarrassment and discomfort. The relief from the admission of my guilt and pain, and the only thing that was holding me back was the fear of not wanting to let go of the past.

As I have said before, a lot of what was caused stemmed from the values I was taught by my parents or mainly a direct cause of my addictions. I tore myself down, admitted all of my wrongs, my faults, exactly who I really am, exactly how bad I really was, my fears my hurts, and all of the people I had harmed. This revelation was a cleansing process for me, dumping my past, admitting my part in my actions, how and what my addiction and thinking lead me to. I admitted exactly who I was and exactly who I am. I forgave myself and accepted my accountability for my actions. By my recognition I know exactly what character defects I have to work on and strive to change to make myself a healthier and better human being. I realize that I don't have to carry garbage around from the past. The past is the past there is absolutely nothing I can do about it. I can only not make those same mistakes again, I can change.

Reflecting back honest humility was something I had very little practice at in the past. I have a sense of great relief in finally being on this journey, a journey that I have known about and attempted in the past but it just was not time for me. I am grateful I made it before I died or spent the rest of my life in jail. I have a willingness to do everything possible for my recovery. I have put my Higher Power first and my recovery second. There was some fear in admitting my faults but with a Higher Power in my life the fear was taken away. I knew a lot of my thinking and my total perception of things had to change, as well as the way I acted and lead my life. I still do wish that what had happened in the past had not gone to the extent it did but I accept that there is nothing but not doing it again can change that.

I feel I have a better understanding of who God is now. It was a spiritual experience and actually the obsessive and compulsive nature of the disease of addiction that I have has lessoned. I have a close contact with my Higher Power, know that he is there working along side of me and guiding me in my recovery and my daily life challenges. I have a conscious contact with my Higher Power I can not explain it but I feel that my Higher Power has great plans for the new way of life I have finally accepted as my gift of recovery. I feel comfort in knowing there is someone who will always listen, and never abandon me.

My self will is of no value what so ever. It got me to exactly where I am today. I have turned my will and my life over to my Higher Power without my Higher Power in my life I could not have made it to this point in my recovery. One of the main things that would take me back to my addiction would be to turn my back, forsake my Higher Power. I feel my Higher Power working in my life and when times of trouble come up in my life, and they will, I know that with the help of my Higher Power I will persevere through it.

Since I have admitted to God, myself and to another human being the exact nature of my wrongs, I have experienced a sense of freedom a sense of relief and healing tranquility, a sense of experiencing serenity, peace of mind. A burden of the past has been taken away and a new freedom of today can be fully experienced.

Step 6

"Were entirely ready to have God remove all these defects of character"

- I am not different, because of the shame I felt I withdrew from society.
- I hid behind the mask I chose. I exposed my true self from everyone.
- My part was not unique, the waste of energy to keep the emotions within me.
- I have created a better and healthier environment for myself and my soul.
- I have a new freedom I have longed for all of my life.

The transition from "was to am"

Serenity

Step1. I am powerless; my life has been dominated by certain emotions.

2 . I am ready to seek help and be delivered out of the confusion of my old ways. I came to believe that a power greater than myself did exist and that, that power would help me should I sought it.

3. I consciously agreed to turn my will and my life over to the care of God.

4&5 .I started cleaning out my emotional closet, and admitted my past to myself, to God and another human being.

I have no guilt and my ego is not trying to draw me back to my old ways of thinking. I turn it over to God and let him be God in me.

Having completed step five I have no areas of doubt about my recovery. My Higher Power works in my life if I turn my will over to him. I do the things suggested to me because I see how it works in other peoples lives and have started to work in mine. I very honestly looked at my resentments, fears, sex conduct, and the people that I have harmed. The energy that was involved in keeping the past covered up overwhelmed me and was a total waste of time. I am on a journey of self discovery, looking at me and my part in the addictions that I am faced with. There may be some things that can be mentioned but these things are not tearing at my soul and causing me to go back to my addiction like in the past.

It seems to be a slow process in having my defects of character removed the physical craving and mental obsession has been taken away and I am realizing my character defects on a daily basis. Take the drugs and alcohol away and the problem (me) is still there. I pray to ask God to remove things. I try to catch myself when my old attitudes and behaviors come up and make amends and learn from my mistakes. I have to be entirely ready to have God remove all my defects of character and the action entirely is the key. I do not have any reservations at all since I have been restored to sanity. When I take even a little bit of my self will back, my desires to do it on my own, my way, I run in absolute conflict with my Higher Power. My Higher Power works in my life when I work it.

These are some of the character defects that in time I'm sure my Higher Power will remove:

- Judgmental
- Impatience
- Controlling
- Anger
- Cynical
- Dishonest
- Evasive
- Liar
- Manipulator
- Greedy
- Inconsiderate
- Intolerant
- Jealously
- Lustful
- Procrastination
- Provocative
- Self centered
- Selfish
- Self Pity
- Vindictive
- Impatient
- With drawn
- Over reactive

I have no reservations that my Higher Power will handle these troubled areas. I have absolutely no reservation since any door open to my justification is a door open to relapse back to hell. I have faith and I work it. I am in conscious contact with my Higher Power through out the day.

I personally know that God is in my life and prayer works when I humble myself before a power greater than myself, and his intension for me. I would not have been able to get past step one in my recovery if it was not for having a Higher Power in my life and turning my will and my life over to him. I get out of self, my self will, because it has done absolutely no good in the past. My whole trouble has been my use and misuse of my will power. I bring my will power into agreement with my God's intention for me. I have a Higher Power in my life and through my Higher Power I have peace and happiness. I have surrendered all of myself to my Higher Power, all of the hurt and the pain, as well as all of the good I totally surrender all every day and every conscious moment that I have. He has taken over my life and it is only when I pray and meditate on a daily basis and consciously turn it over to him, he works in my life when I allow him to. When I take back even a little bit of my self will I see problems starting to surface again in my life. I am ready willing and able with honesty, open mindedness. I do the best I can and willingness comes from turning it over and accepting my Higher Power in my life. It works for me and I see the promises of recovery on a daily basis. I pray and ask God to remove my character defects on a daily basis.

Some of these character defects I exult in and do love, for example.

Selfishness - I have to look out for myself first
Dishonesty - Sometimes the truth can hurt another person

Controlling - I can know best at times
Judgmental - It protects me from harm

These are the character defects that I am not willing to completely give up yet. I know that I must deal with all my character defects but I see positive as well as negative qualities in these defects.

God loves me even through all of my faults and my shortcomings. He loves me as an addict and a recovering addict. It is against Gods will to be active and self destructive in my addiction. God knows what is best for me and will lead me on the right path and as long as I do not turn my back on God he will love me and keep me from harm. I am humbled through his action of his mercy and grace.

I have self esteem today where I did not have it in my addiction. By turning it over and relying on my Higher Power this gives me new hope that I am a good person deserving of a better and more satisfying life. I have humility, modesty, freedom from pride, self regard for my feeling of my own qualities and accomplishments. I humble myself before something that is all powerful and knowing and all seeing. I have let go of all of my past my pain and my hurts. I have left a clean slate and have let God chose the path in recovery I will take. I am excited in the knowledge that God will be joining me on my journey. I have hope and a new freedom that I never had before. I feel an overwhelming presence of a power greater than myself. I have a feeling of wholeness. I have happiness that I have always longed for. I have new directions and attainable goals. I have a feeling of well being and have a closer contact with God and know that he is working in my life.

My whole idea of being in recovery is to change absolutely every thing about myself. Everything in my addiction, my beliefs, ideas, attitudes and behaviors got me to exactly where it was meant to get me, Insane on the street, homeless, family giving up, jail, sick, hospitals and suicidal. My old mind sets are of no use to me in recovery. By reassigning absolutely everything about me, almost everything had to be changed. I had to unlearn old attitudes and ways of looking at things and practice the knowledge that I have learned. I am enjoying the new life and have chosen to see the benefit of my new lifestyle that I have chosen.

A must to do list:

Go to meetings, I go when I want to, I go when I do not want to and I go all of the other times.
Get a home group and sponsor
Work the steps honestly
Do service work
Fellowship, no using people in my life, places and things
Journal daily
Share my experience, strength and hope
Strengthen my conscious contact with my Higher Power
When I get into a situation and I get a gut feeling or my recovery is in jeopardy, step back, question reassess, pray and ask opinion of two other people
Do not fall into old attitudes and behaviors, thinking, justifying and rationalizing

ABSOLUTELY UNDER ANY AND ALL CONDITIONS NO MATTER WHAT, DO NOT USE

RECOVERY-HIGHER POWER-TOM

The program of AA has many tools and slogans that help and strengthen me. These are a few examples.

First things first
Easy does it
Think, think, think
Just for today
The past is history

Total change
Faith without works is dead
I am a sick person getting healthier
Insanity is a state of addiction
I can always be worse
Dis-ease
It is OK
Live in the present
Recovery is first in my life
Restless, irritable, discontent
The truth will set you free
Play the tape to the end
Those weird mental blank spots
Live in the solution instead of the problem
Let go let God
Practice these principles in all of my affairs
Accepting of all people, places, and things
I can only change myself
God's grace is sufficient
We are spiritual people having a physical experience
100% conviction, no back door
I love myself and deserve recovery

Change the attitude and the behavior will follow
The promises are happening
Turn it over
Put good in and get good out
It's a game of inches
It does get better
It is my choice
Do not believe the lie
Stinking thinking
Mental, physical, emotional, spiritual
Jails, institutions and death
Spiritual awakening
Solution-you-beliefs-behaviors
I am only as sick as my secrets
God is at the centre of my recovery
Give up in order to receive
Lose in order to win
Honest humility
The journey of a thousand miles starts with the first step
I take responsibility for my own life
Honesty, openness willingness
Willingness, foundation to spiritual freedom
Love-genuine care and concern
Prayer and meditation
My needs are met my wants are just bonuses
Stupid people do stupid things and stupid things have consequences
When all else seams to fail there is always recovery
Never say never

The most affective way to turn to God as I understand him is prayer and meditation, keeping my Higher Power first in my recovery, turning over my will and my life. This is the spiritual basis of my program.

I have already experienced an improvement in myself. I have a change in attitude and behavior. I am more caring, and have a genuine concern for other people. I am less judgmental and have judgment. Patience and tolerance are my attributes. I have accepted people, places and things for what they are and have a new found hope. I have gratitude for recovery and the little things in my life. I am a lot more open, willing and honest. I do not steal, cheat or lie, and when I am in doubt I do check it out. The answer was and is recovery acceptance, amends and accountability.

Step 7

"Humbling asked him to remove our shortcomings"

My definition of humbling myself is character building. Spiritual values had to come first and materiel satisfactions were not the purpose of living. Honest and morality, character building, tolerance and true love of man and God, the daily basis of living, the true purpose of our lives. We need to be true and honest about ourselves, to ourselves and others. Through humility we grow and serve others. It is though service to others and sharing that our problems diminish.

Humility is at work in my life today,

- I admit that I am an alcoholic and addict to myself and others.
- I openly pray and meditate.
- I admit when I am wrong and ask for directions.
- I give when someone is in need

- I help my fellow man, give of myself, without asking anything in return.
- I seek out a better relationship with my Higher Power instead of material processions.
- I admit my faults and shortcomings and character defects.
- I admit that I am powerless over my addiction and that my life is unmanageable.
- I am far from perfect and I do not strive for perfection.
- I turn my will and my life over to my Higher Power.
- I look for the good in everything.
- I admit my wrongs and the harms I have done in the past.

I have a sense of relief and contentment in knowing that my Higher Power is in control and that I have turned my will and my life over. I have serenity, peace and happiness and know that my Higher Power is directing me on the right path. The disease has liberated me from the past.

I am willing to accept he fact that I cannot change some things.

- I cannot change the past or undo the things that I have done.
- I cannot change the fact that I have a criminal record.
- I have burnt a lot of bridges when it comes to nursing jobs.
- Attitudes and lack of respect and trust of people from the past.
- The things that I have done to my family – I am not in control.

- The assaults and criminal activities.
- My behavior and abuse towards Debbie.
- My lack of being a father with Devon when I was in my addiction.
- The money I have spent and the material processions I do not have.

There is absolutely nothing in the past that has happened that I can change. The past is the past what has been done has been done. I can not go back into the past and change it if I could I would. I have accepted my mistakes in the past and made myself accountable for my actions. I turn it over to my Higher Power I do not dwell in the past or live in the past. Today is the only day that holds any importance to me and with my Higher Power I will get through it. I have abandoned the old me in total favor of the new me in recovery. I know that with my conscious contact with my Higher Power that I will be “”OK” My Higher Power is not going to give me any thing more than I can handle. My life has changed around for the better, exactly opposite from what I was.

I pray and meditate on a daily basis. I ask for patience and tolerance, I ask for others and little of myself. I ask for help when I am in decision I step back and ask for help. I know that through my willingness I have gained independence, I ask for the power to heal me and set me free from the bondage of addiction and that way I can help others. I let God heal my soul.

I have a new outlook on life and look at things a lot differently. I have a new perspective on who I am and what I am doing here. I am in recovery because my Higher Power did not put me here to be an alcoholic and a drug addict. I have done a lot of work mentally, spiritually, and emotionally on this fantastic journey that I am on. Life is not difficult as I thought it was in the past. It is a challenge at times and I accept that fact. It is like this big heavy cloud that has been hanging over me for years, has been lifted from me. I see a new light with a new outlook and a feeling of contentment.

These are some of the repeated humilities that forced me to learn about humility.

- Admitting honestly on a daily basis that I am an alcoholic and drug addict.
- Knowing that even though life is going on around me I can only do what I can do today.
- That I only have recovery just for today.
- What I have done in the past, I have accepted, and others still might have problems with my past I accept that.
- Recovery is a long and involved process.
- There is a lot of work to be done.
- People will look down upon me because I am an addict and I accept that.
- There are a lot of amends I have to make to the people that I have harmed.
- It just takes one drink or drug to go back to the hell I came from and it is my choice to make that.
- I humble myself before God and pray and meditate on a daily basis.

There are many parts of my old behavior and personality that refuse to be changed. I constantly work on it and it is a process of recovery that will take time and time is the mender of a lot of my problems. Change cannot happen over night, like my recovery it is a total process of change on a daily basis. From time to time I see old behavior patterns surfacing, procrastination, being lazy, criticizing and being judgmental, anger, knowing better, being uptight and flying off the handle letting things get to me. I have to remember I can not control the situation or the person. I have to remember to turn it over.

I now have a new found freedom. I have to be on top of it all at all times, always aware of my surroundings, my feeling and in conscious contact with my Higher Power. I have no fear about my new freedom because I know and feel my Higher Power in my life. I try to always be aware of my surroundings and what is going on inside of me. I do not allow anything to jeopardize my sobriety. I can be afraid at times and I accept that. My recovery comes first and every thing is second.

Humility is necessary to my survival. I humble myself before my Higher Power. I get out of myself and help others instead of being so selfish like in my addiction. I admit my faults and my short comings, my wrongs and my mistakes. To be humble in my actions gives me serenity and peace in my life.

I find that I am more content with myself today. I actually love myself and look at things in a positive way. I am comfortable in my own skin and enjoy being alone with myself. I like where I am today. I have goals in my life, ambitions and see the whole picture of where I was and where I am today.

There have been a number of times in recovery that I have been faced with major problems in my life that would have normally kept me in my addiction, or have sent me on a well known spree.

- Problems at home / family life
- Going off my anti-depressants
- Personal conflict in the treatment house
- My dishonesty

I have a level of accepting of people, places and things as being exactly the way they are and supposed to be. I have run into adversity in my recovery but anything is just a plan of my Higher Power, I go with the flow and have little idea of what the big picture is. Pain is the admission price to new life.

I react in a different manner towards life. I have a better understanding of things and especially myself. I do not get all bent out of shape like I used to and I do not let things bother me and cause me to relapse like they used to. I accept people, places and things exactly as they should be. I can not control situations and people like I use to. Life is a lot better and more rewarding in recovery and I am grateful for what I have instead of what I don't have. When a situation arises I take a step back, try to assess the situation, reevaluate and try to accept it. I have learned that if I over react I am taking my will back not God's will, and usually it is not as bad as what I make it out to be and I am usually wrong about the situation. So instead of putting my self through a lot of wasted energy I can either walk away or deal with it as quickly as possible, time out, walk away.

Today I have been able to remodel old liabilities into assets.

- My energy in doing something.
- My attitude of half assed measures availed me nothing.
- Being good at what I can do.
- I have a sense of perfectionism.

- I can be a loner but I am comfortable with myself.
- I was not so good at maintaining my addiction but I have learned what to do in my recovery.

In the past fear has robbed me of a lot but I am learning to deal with it now.

Fear of success - I'm looking at schooling bettering myself.

Fear of being part of my family-looking at counseling and acceptance.

Fear of moving on. - Have goals for the future, moving to the Interior.

Fear of sharing and making friends-I'm more open and sharing and meeting people.

Fear of the unknown-I try new things and experiences.

Fear of not being knowledgeable-learning more about myself and recovery.

Fear of being accepted-more honest, open and willing.

Fear of being to self centered-trying to get out of self, being selfless.

By my admission of my powerlessness, accepting and turning my life over to a Higher Power, making and sharing a list of my wrongs and the people I have harmed, looking at my character defects and asking God to remove my short comings I am that much closer on my spiritual journey and closer with my conscious contact with my Higher Power. God does work with me in my life when I allow him to and do not take my self will back. I am the problem and live in the solution in recovery and faith.

Step 8

Beginning of the end of isolation.

"Made a list of all the people we had harmed and became willing to make amends to them all."

I am very glad that the light of truth made its way through my illusions to capture my attention.

These are some of the people I would like to make amends to:

God:

- For not following your way and at one time turning my back on you.
- For breaking your commandments, stealing, lying, and hurting people, hurting myself.
- For not having a conscious contact with you.
- For not recognizing when you were there giving me support and direction.
- For forsaking you.

Me:

- For not loving myself.
- For allowing me to do the things I did.
- For being an alcoholic and a drug addict.
- For not making goals, keeping promises and for procrastination.
- For not living life to my full potential.
- Not being a proper father to Devon or a partner to Debbie.
- For all the people I hurt physically and mentally.
- For hurting myself and trying to give up on life.
- For not trying harder when I knew I could change.

Dad:

- For not maintaining any contact.
- For wanting you dead.
- For fighting and stealing from you.
- For not accepting the fact that all you knew is what your father taught you.
- For not being the son that you wanted.
- For not understanding you.

Mom:

- For physically and emotionally abusing you.
- Lying when I was in my addiction about needing money.
- For making you worry about me, my lack of contact and your feelings about what you have gone through.
- Not respecting your wishes and your son grew up to be an alcoholic and addict.

My sister:

- For not being with you when your daughter was still born.
- For turning my back on you.
- For not maintaining contact with you.
- For hurting you physically, emotionally and mentally.

Others:

- Stealing from the many places I worked at, computer, ring, phone, money, drugs,
- Stealing from the government.

In looking back at my past faults and the people I have harmed and making an attempt to repair the damage I have done, I will have cleared away the shit of the past, the things that I have been carrying around with me that had caused all of my guilt and shame. This process will enable me to develop the best possible relationships with every human being that I know. I am truly beginning to see how stuffing down my shame, anger and resentments has affected my future. These are emotions that have caused a great deal of problems in my life. The more I have, the more I drink and use drugs, and the more hurt I cause other people. These things have to be dealt with if I am going to keep my recovery.

Shame:
This was put upon me by my father and saying that I was worthless and unwanted. The life style I lead brought the shame upon me, being an alcoholic and a junkie.

Anger:
I have always been an angry person, thinking that the world owed me and I should get my own way. I was angry at myself for what I had become, a hopeless addict and I took it out on other people especially the ones that I loved and cared for me.

Resentments:
The people that I thought had harmed me and how I hated these people for that. How I had hurt myself and others and how sick I felt over the whole thing. How I felt that people were in the way of my dreams, if any, which were mostly imagined.

I have hurt people physically, mentally and emotionally. I have put people down, assaulted people, hurt feelings, lost trust. People had given up hope on me. I know that I am a good person, caring, loving and understanding. I am selfless and compassionate. When I add alcohol and drugs to this I turn into a totally evil person. I become very selfish and self centered not caring who I hurt, what I do or who I use in order to get what I want. I have no morals or conscience in my actions.

When I make amends I honestly admit my part and how I have hurt that person. I make myself accountable for my actions and I do not have to carry the guilt and shame around with me any more. I erase the slate clean, new start on my new life in recovery. It means that I can develop the best possible relationship with people in the future.

I would also feel good if someone I loved came to me to make amends for some harm done to me.

- My father: he could admit his wrongs and tell me that he loves me, cares for me and respects me, that

he is proud of me and is sorry for the things he said and did when I was growing up.
- My mother: If she could give me credit for where I am in my life, that she tried the best she could when I was growing up and that she is sorry for not getting out of her relationship with my father.
- My sister: For putting me down, not understanding what I was doing in my addiction.

I hurt myself the most and work at forgiving me, first, in the shame and guilt I had for myself and how I had hit the self destruct button on my life and hurt a lot of people, defected relationships due to my addictions. By forgiving myself I can gain forgiveness from others. Thoroughness will pay off in the end.

I am aware that my self will has affected others in many drastic ways. I wanted to totally run the show. I have the willingness to go to any lengths and no fear because I have a Higher Power in my life and it is his will for me to feel a lightening of my anxieties when beginning to forgive others. I know that through the course of making amends I will grow from isolation and closer to God. I pray for the willingness to make amends and received it.

I do feel a comfort in knowing God has forgiven me. In step three I turned my will and my life over to the care of my Higher Power, he has forgiven me for my wrongs and I feel a sense of relief in that.

Today I have forgiven people who have harmed me, made mistakes or judgments against me. I try to accept people, places and things for what they are. I make amends when I do a wrong to someone else and admit my part. All I can do is not make those same mistakes again. It has to be done in order to recover.

It is becoming clear to me that the characteristics I dislike in others are sometimes mirrored in my own personality. It makes me humbler in the relationships that for so many years I thought insanely that I was better than someone else. We are all the same in the eyes of God.

I have the willingness to make amends and know that in making them I will become a much better person in the process. This is not going to be accomplished overnight in no means. It is a long and involved process. I can not rush this and amends will be made when they come up.

My silent shadow voice is becoming clearer to me. My Higher Power makes things known to me more indirectly. I am totally amazed that when a question does come up the answer is shown to me. I just have to be open to it and I will hear.

I am learning to avoid making extreme judgments about others and learning to take a more objective view. I look at it as eying and yang. Everyone has good in them with a little bad. No one is perfect only God holds the right to perfection in all. I look at the good in people instead of the bad, since anything bad can be changed if the willingness is there. I share what I have learned with others since I can not keep this gift unless I give it away.

Step 9

"Made direct amends to such people wherever possible, except when to do so would injure them or others"

I am starting to feel I have good judgment and more careful sense of timing, courage and prudence. I have all these things because I have a Higher Power in my life and I trust in my Higher Power to lead me in the right direction. Things are working out, my judgment is getting better. I look at things more carefully. The whole process of recovery is change and looking at those things that need to be accomplished.

What making a direct amends means to me is going to the person with sincerity, admitting my harm to them. The goal is to pay the price necessary to get free of the past so I can live to my fullest capacity. It takes a great deal of courage but the pay off is well worth it. For me to go about making amends it is important that I have thoroughly done the first seven steps. I have the support of friends in recovery and my sponsor. I do not make amends to gain forgiveness I'm paying the price to get free from the past once and for all. The amends process will be a long time talking to each person personally and having time in between to recuperate from the stress of each encounter. I want to understand the thoughts and feelings associated with each encounter. My amends process is a growth process, a freeing process. I can not do it impulsively but listen each time what is exactly happening to me in the process.

I see now where forgiveness can set me free and heal my past memories. I have been carrying this plate of shit around with me so long and I have had a tremendous amount of guilt, shame and remorse. I know that making an amends will heal the past. This whole process of recovery is a healing process and I must heal and have the willingness in order to recover.

I admit the harms that I have done to other people and make myself accountable for my actions. I forgive the people who have harmed me since most of their actions are a direct result of my actions towards them. I have to forgive myself in order to forgive others. I can not live in the past like I use to since the feeling surrounding the past caused me to relapse.

I pray each morning for patience, tolerance and understanding. I pray for forgiveness for what ever harms I may commit during the day and for the amends I make and how I can learn from my actions. Through the previous steps I am decreasing the gap between my Higher Power and myself.

I will have a conscious contact with my Higher Power before I make any decision and go with what my Higher Power tells me to do. I ask for direction and receive it when I have the open mindedness. As long as I don't take my self will back I will be OK in the amends I have to make for my recovery.

By first admitting the reality of my addiction and the problems it has caused for other people would be of major significance to people especially my family. Even though they know most of the circumstances surrounding my addiction I don't think they know the mental and emotional part of it or the major steps I have taken to changing, becoming a better healthier person and my conviction in my recovery.

For the most part I do not have difficulty making amends. I know that when I am wrong I do promptly admit it and move on but there are those times for certain things in the past (criminal), the thought of a severe penalty comes to mind. I do not want to live in a problem for the moment and can see the value in owning my part and moving on. In making amends I fix what I have broken, period, that is what my aim is to do. Certain amends for now require that I take an indirect approach. In the future I hope that more willingness will be there and a satisfying more direct approach will be taken.

I have determined which people I will make amends to in person. My immediate family will be quite understanding of the process and the sincere desire.

- Myself
- Debbie
- Devon
- Adam
- Debbie's family-
- Mom
- Donna
- Traci
- Sharon
- Wayne
- My family-

- Mom
- Dad?
- My sister
- My uncle

There are some people I may have to make an amends to by mail.

- My father-distance if not eventually in person
- Bill-If I know his where about

I will approach the amends with and attitude of quiet sincerity. I will explain the changes I have made in my life and the stance that I have in my recovery. That I was a very sick person in my addiction and that I was wrong and will fix whatever harm I have done. I will have the honesty, open mindedness and willingness to fix the harm that I have done in the past.

Words alone can not express how I feel about my journey so far. It is beyond my wildest dreams; something that I am living that I did not think was attainable. It shows me that I can do something when I have the willingness to do it and that my goals and dreams do come true. I found the happiness that has always been covered up by my addiction. With my Higher Power in my life dreams do come true. I cannot predict the outcome I just know that lessons will be learned and no harm will come to me. I have a new freedom that I have never had before. I have love and compassion and can greet each day with a new vigor that I have never had before. I admit my wrongs without living in yesterday. This is the start of my journey and I have to continue to do the things that I know work for me today.

Step 10

"Continued to take personal inventory and when we were wrong promptly admitted it"

I take an inventory on a daily basis. I continuously look at my assets and liabilities in order to grow by these means. This unsparing self-survey and criticism can become a regular habit where I can admit and accept what I find and patiently and persistently try to correct what is wrong. When my old feelings of anger, fear, jealousy, my negative emotions, those that jeopardize my peace of mind and serenity, come up I realize that it is the old addict talking in me again. If a situation arises, a question, if it is good for my recovery I admit and correct my errors right away so I can settle it and get on with the day. It is usually something that is so small in nature and I have blown out of proportion. I realize exactly what had started it all off and I fix It that moment.

Life is very precious to me now in recovery. It has meaning and is to be cherished. I know now who I am and that my Higher Power does have a plan for me. That plan I only get a glimpse of from time to time. Life is a journey, something to be lived and enjoyed. It is very precious moment by moment. Life is a constant chance, ever new, learning and exciting.

I feel the comfort in receiving the day and taking stock of my activities, and being watchful for circumstances that need to be corrected. I try to learn from all, or any of my mistakes I make during the day. By learning from these mistakes I can grow in my recovery. I try to make it a regular part of my day being in the early part of my recovery, the early stages old behaviors and attitudes do come up from time to time. It is through these learning experiences I become better, healthier and happier.

I am more open and expressive now. In a lot of situations I need self-restraint, honest analysis of what is involved and the willingness to admit when the fault is mine and make amends accordingly. I do not carry the same loud of jealousy envy, self-pity, or pride around with me like I did in the past. I try to address the situation openly and express my feelings instead of carrying it into the next day. I am recognizing my old ways before they take over. When I speak or act hastily or rashly, when I am not fair minded or patient/tolerant, unkind, judgmental, quick tempered, prideful, vengeful, take a piece of my self will back or when I'm not doing what I have to do for my recovery today. These are old traits of my old addict coming back wanting to lead me down the road to a final destination of relapse.

Sometimes it can be difficult around family. This is my greatest challenge. I realized that I had to forgive myself first for the wrongs that I committed in my addiction. I realize that it will and may never be that other people will forgive me the same way. I have changed a lot of my old ways and have learned a new way of living. I have to practice a lot of patience and tolerance around this because even though I needed a life threatening issue to bring about my change, they do not necessarily require the same thing. I hope that with time they might decide to change because they see what I have done as being attractive enough for them to want to change.

There are some that do not know how to communicate with me now. I have a choice today to be around the people that I want to be around, especially the people who are a threat to my recovery. Some people have a hard time accepting a person with a positive attitude and outlook upon life. I am me, my own person I can be and show kindness and love toward my fellow man. At times I can be confused and hurt or not understanding of how a person feels towards me. All I can do is accept that person for what they believe and not change their opinion of me. Acceptance is the key to all my problems today ever reminding me to place principles before personalities.

Occasionally I find myself reverting back to my old ways. It always happens when I take a little piece of my self will back and start living life according to Tom and not my Higher Power's will for me. I can run around with my head cut off, in circles with to much to do and too little time to do it, always doing it the hardest most difficult way, not taking the time to think things through. I express these feelings to another person which takes all the power out of the situation, step back and reassess.

Each day I am setting aside time to discuss my day with my Higher Power. In the morning I give thanks for the start of the day and ask that one of my character defects be taken away. I plan the day but not the outcome. During the day

I take a spot check inventory of how the day is progressing and how I am feeling and if my day is progressing on the right path. At night I give thanks again and do a check. I try the next day to right my wrongs I did and make sure I do not make those same mistakes again.

I have a support system in place in my recovery today. I do not keep things all bottled up like I did in the past. I am more open and honest than ever before. By talking to someone the power is taken away about what I am feeling at that moment. I have a conscious contact with my Higher Power and people in my life I can share my feelings and troubles with, people at meetings, people who are in recovery.

There are parts of my old personality that are more persistent than others. The old addict behavior and attitude comes upon me on numerous occasions, my controlling nature, my impatience, getting my wants met and my total persistence over anything else.

I try to keep myself in check on a regular basis because I know that not doing so could take me back to the hopeless slow death of my addiction. It is a slow process and the willingness is there to try and better myself and be the person that my Higher Power wants me to be. I am sincere and ask every day for God to remove my short comings. I look at my motives of most thoughts and actions that appear wrong. How I could have done better and how I would have been treated if I were on the other end of it. I can not rationalize my actions, my motives and reasons. Having considered all of these things I have done well. I can truly thank my Higher Power and sleep in good conscience.

Step II

"Sought through prayer and meditation to improve our conscious contact with God, as we understand him, praying only for knowledge of his will for us and the power to carry that out"

Self examination, meditation and prayer are very important in my life as a recovering addict. This is my new foundation for life. I am given direction either directly or usually indirectly. I want to live life to the fullest, and in the process I am given the opportunity to help my fellow addict.

Thy will be done in my life not mine:

I am conscious of the people in my environment and how they interact in my life. I am more conscious of my feelings and thoughts and how my will interferes with the will of God and others. I do not force my will upon others. There is a balance that I try to maintain and am seeking to maintain it. It is God's will for me and the power to carry that out. I do what I need to do and not what I want to do.

When ever I have doubt in my mind I don't do it. When there are doubts I am not following God's will for me. My self-will got me into the hell of my addiction and left me feeling hopeless and helpless, full of shame and guilt. At times I take a little bit of my self-will back and let the old addict attitudes and behaviors come back. I can get to the point where I want every thing done according to Tom's will and Tom's life. When I am feeling uncomfortable and bent out of shape. It is only through prayer and meditation that I gain the knowledge of his will for me and the courage to carry that out.

Step 12

"Having had a spiritual awakening as a result of these steps we tried to carry the message to alcoholics and to practice the principles in all of our affairs"

Tom fulfilled his dream to move to the Interior and continued to share his story in the AA rooms of Penticton for over a year. He succeeded in getting a job working in a nursing home. He bought a new car and had a nice home with his family. Tom brought Debbie's oldest son to recovery when he was 19 years old; he just turned 31 and has been clean and sober for 11 years. Tom touched many people on his journey to recovery.

One night after Tom had finished a 3pm to 11pm shift at work he did not come home, instead he made the choice to go out and score cocaine and he started his journey back to hell all over again. His family was torn apart. He tried several times to get back on the right track but was not successful. Months later Devon and I moved back to Victoria. The Big Book of AA tells us jails, institutes, and deaths are the result of alcohol and drug addiction. As Tom has shared with us in his story he certainly did experience these things. Sadly on September 6th, 2000 Tom committed suicide as a result of this horrifying disease. Tom shined in his sobriety God only knows the reason he made that choice to go back out there. The twelve step program worked for him when he was working the program. Tom is greatly missed by his family.

Tom taking his own life has been one of the greatest tragedies of my life. If it wasn't for my Higher Power, The Lord Jesus Christ, I never would have made it through those first years. Some thing like this is not anything you ever get over you just learn to cope. Tom spoke many times in his story on how he had attempted suicide in his addiction and always had suicidal thoughts. He was treated for depression but chose to go off all drugs including his medication. I often wonder if this story would have ended so sadly if he had of remained on his medication.

Drug addiction and suicide are very often connected. Drug addiction can cause depression leading to suicide and people who suffer from depression sometimes use drugs and alcohol to suppress there sad feelings. Whether it is the substance abuse that is the cause of the depression, or the depression that is the cause of the substance abuse, complete abstinence from drugs and alcohol helps in the prevention of suicide attempts.

Substance abuse alters brain chemistry. Thoughts become irrational and reality goes right out the window when under the influence. A number of negative thoughts can take over while under the influence of drugs and alcohol.

It is sad that so many people who chose to end their own life do not seek professional help in the days and weeks prior to making that rash and final decision. Rarely does anyone know the whole story of drug addiction suicide. Tom enjoyed his sobriety and I'm grateful for the time we had. The program of AA teaches us how drugs and alcohol are" Cunning, Baffling and Powerful". Jesus said in the bible in John 10:10 The thief comes only to steal and kill and destroy; I have come that they may have life, and have it to the full.

I just pray that anyone reading Tom's story will be inspired to get help. If you or a loved one is suffering from addictions you must seek help. Suicide is not the answer, don't believe the lie. There is hope and a healthy sober life can be obtained, one day at a time.

Not Saying Goodbye

Waiting to see the peace and tranquility in
your face as you sleep,
Wanting to caress you, though shall not weep,
Wanting to come over and hold you so,
Afraid of the pain, not wanting to let go,
And so I leave not saying goodbye,
Though I'm breaking inside, I will not deny.

This is just the beginning not another end,
So I wish you well and take care, my beautiful,
beautiful friend.

In loving memory of Tom June 5th,
1962-September 6th, 2000

Debbie and Devon